Becoming a
MARKETING NINJA

A-Z Guide to Fast-Track Your
Marketing Career for Newbies

Authors Tree®
PUBLISHING

Becoming a
MARKETING NINJA

Cover designed by **Authors Tree Publishing**, image used from free stock library.
ISBN: 978-93-94807-99-0
India: INR 399/-
Outside India: $ 7.99 USD

Authors Tree Publishing
W/13, Aman Vihar, BSP
Pin: 495001
Call: +91 9109886656
www.authorstree.com
First Edition. 2024

Printed In India

Becoming a MARKETING NINJA

A-Z Guide to Fast-Track Your Marketing Career for Newbies

Written By

N. KANNAN

Manufacturers 3X Growth Consultant

To my father,

Late Shri V. Natarajan,

*whose wisdom (and vast collection of hand-written quotes) I
look up to even today.*

Contents

Acknowledgement

I extend my sincere acknowledgements to Mr. Murali Sundaram, the visionary founder of the 'Teachers are Leaders Community (TLC)', and Mr. A. Gunasekaran, Head of Training and Franchise Operations, TLC. Their unwavering encouragement and guidance bolstered my confidence to embark on the journey of penning my debut book.

I am deeply grateful to Mr. Sunil Pande, my esteemed senior and mentor at L&T, for graciously agreeing to contribute a foreword to my book.

I also express my deep gratitude to Mr. Rajanbabu Govindan, my cousin and Ex-MD of Litens Automotive, for agreeing to write a Foreword to my book.

A special tribute goes to my dedicated editing team, comprising my daughter Shruti Kannan, Jaya Srinivasan, and G. Subramanian. Their tireless efforts over many days ensured that my readers would derive maximum benefit from the content.

I also extend heartfelt thanks to my friend, Dr. Shanker Viswanath for his valuable assistance in copy-editing and proofreading my book.

I am also thankful to my niece, Anjali Chandrashekar, and daughter Shruti for their assistance in the selection of the book cover.

I reserve a special appreciation for my wife, Padma, and my family- son, Siddharth, daughter-in-law, Vaidehi, and son-in-law, Shreyas- for being unwavering pillars of strength and support throughout the writing process. In addition, I am grateful to my grandson, Vishrut, whose infectious energy always keeps me refreshed.

Lastly, I express my gratitude to my publisher, Authors Tree Publishing, for bringing forth this wonderful book for my readers.

Foreword

It is with great pleasure that I pen down a few words for N. Kannan's upcoming book, **"Becoming a Marketing Ninja"** and I can assure you that this will be an informative and engaging read.

Marketing is a fascinating and ever-changing field. What is an effective marketing technique today, may not even be a relevant one tomorrow. One would need to have a good blend of creative and analytical thinking to understand how to pitch a product to a customer and show them that it is exactly what they are looking for. A good marketer would need to have in-depth knowledge of the product, possess the ability to read people accurately, exhibit good communication skills and be willing to go the extra mile for the team and the customer. I have seen Kannan exhibit these values over my long association with him, and have witnessed firsthand the dedication, strategic insight, and innovative thinking that define his approach to marketing.

My association with Kannan began in the 90s when he was a part of my team at L&T Eutectic, where we worked on the marketing of Eutectic Products. Over a working relationship of 33 years continuing into a friendship till date, I have seen Kannan's brilliant communication and marketing skills translate prospective customers into revenue for the company.

Kannan's unique perspective, honed by years of experience and a genuine passion for the field, offers invaluable information on marketing. In this book, Kannan has elaborated upon several topics ranging from how to create a marketing strategy and develop a brand image, all the way to marketing in the digital realm. He has researched these topics well and combining that with his experience in this field has resulted in a one-stop compilation of everything that you would need to get started with marketing in today's world.

Whether you are a 'newbie' just starting in this field, or the owner of a small business seeking to develop effective marketing strategies or a seasoned professional looking to keep up with the latest developments in this field, this book will be an essential resource for you.

Best Wishes,
Sunil Pande
Ex-Senior VP & Country Manager (USA), L&T Infotech
Ex-Executive VP & Board member, L&T Power

Foreword

It is both a personal joy and a source of professional pride for me to write the Foreword for the book **"Becoming a Marketing Ninja"** by N. Kannan, my cousin and longtime marketing professional.

I have primarily worked in Operations, but found myself thrust into the role of Business Development Director when launching a new MNC in Pune fifteen years ago. My discussions with Kannan during the initial stages of this challenge helped me understand the Marketing Mantra shared by him in his own distinctive and straightforward manner. In the realm of organisational dynamics, it is interesting to see that usually the Purchasing and Project teams are given more power in decision making, and the Marketing team is seemingly powerless. It is an open secret that Marketing is what fuels business and financial success for any organisation, but only the marketing guy knows that - he holds the least authoritative position within the company but has to deftly handle both internal management and customer relationships and keep both teams happy, while also meeting both their business objectives.

It is fitting that Kannan advocates for readers to become Marketing Ninjas, as mastery of this field is a nonnegotiable requirement for a successful business. The reader is fortunate to have the essence of various skill sets explained so well in this book, along with guidance on understanding the ever-evolving landscape of innovations in this field.

Regardless of the reader's current standing in the profession, I am confident that they will benefit immensely from this book, as Kannan extensively covers the diverse requirements of marketing at all levels.

I extend my best wishes to Kannan for his endeavour in imparting his wisdom to the Marketing fraternity.

Rajanbabu Govindan
Ex Managing Director,
Litens Automotive I Pvt Ltd, Pune.

Introduction

In the fast-paced arena of modern business, where information flows like a river, and trends change as swiftly as the wind, a breed of professionals has mastered the art of influence, persuasion, and connection. They are the "Marketing Ninjas", or people who excel in marketing. Welcome to a journey that will transform you from a marketing novice into a Marketing Ninja, wielding the tools of the trade with precision and finesse.

In the digital age, where every click, like, and share can make or break a brand, the role of a marketer has evolved into something akin to that of a martial artist. It requires knowledge, agility, creativity, and the ability to adapt swiftly. **"Become a Marketing Ninja: An A-Z Guide to Fast-Track Your Marketing Career for Newbies"** is your **Dojo** (place for immersive learning or experiential learning), and I am your **Sensei** (teacher or mentor), here to guide you through the intricacies of modern marketing.

As we know it today, marketing is far from its humble beginnings. It has transcended billboards and TV ads, leaping into the boundless realms of the internet, social media, data analytics, and beyond. This transformation has created unprecedented opportunities for those ready to learn and adapt.

Are you a newcomer to the marketing world, eager to carve a niche for yourself in this dynamic field? Or perhaps you're a seasoned marketer looking to sharpen your skills and stay ahead of the curve. Regardless of your background or experience, this book is designed to be your compass, training manual, and secret weapon in the marketing world.

We will journey through the entire marketing landscape, starting with the fundamentals, targeting the right audience, delving into digital marketing strategies, content creation, social media management, and everything in between. We will decode the mystery of SEO (Search Engine Optimization), demystify the magic of branding, and harness the power of nurturing relationships to captivate your audience and make them loyal to your brand. Each chapter has relevant real-world examples of successful companies in their marketing efforts to help you grasp the concept.

But remember, becoming a Marketing Ninja is not just about acquiring knowledge; it's about embodying a mindset that thrives on innovation, embraces change, and believes in the power of influence to make a difference. This will result in "scaling up" your business by implementing strategies for sustained growth and long-term success.

So, prepare yourself for a transformational journey through the world of marketing. Along the way, you will unlock the secrets, strategies, and tactics with relevant examples that will empower you to fast-track your marketing career and become a true Marketing Ninja. Let's embark on this journey together, and by the end of it, you'll hopefully have not just knowledge or skills but also a mindset to conquer the marketing battlefield and emerge as a Marketing Ninja.

Chapter 1

LAYING THE FOUNDATION: A NEWBIE'S ORIENTATION

"The aim of marketing is to know and understand the customer so well the product or service fits them and sells itself." **- Peter Drucker**

The term 'Marketing' involves promoting and selling products or services, as well as conducting market research and advertising. The goal is to offer something of value to customers, clients, partners, and society.

The Marketing department is the public face of a company, responsible for coordinating and creating all materials that represent the business. Their role is to reach out to prospective customers, investors, or the community while creating a favourable image of the company and presenting it positively.

Market research is necessary to ensure that a company makes the right decisions. This process helps in understanding the marketplace, including identifying unmet needs and determining how to capitalise on opportunities that are not being served. Market research encompasses studying competitors, identifying key demographics, determining prices, and devising optimal promotions to attract customers. The term 'demographics' includes factors like location, age, education level, income, or occupation which can be used to segment a market into groups.

Marketing Management involves strategizing, implementing, and monitoring an organisation's marketing approach. This covers the marketing plan, campaigns, and tactics employed to generate and fulfil the demand of specific customers, aiming to boost profitability.

Marketing Strategy

A marketing strategy shows how a business plans to get people interested and attract customers towards its products or services. This includes market research, branding, distribution channels, advertising, and pricing.

Using a mix of 'pull' and 'push' marketing strategies is advisable.

'Push advertising' aims to push products toward specific customers, for example, new companies marketing their products through paid social media ads or billboards.

'Pull advertising', on the other hand, aims to draw customers to your products; for example, a company might try to make itself visible to its target market by using search engine optimization or create a blog that a prospective customer might read to make an informed choice.

Five Key Elements for an Effective Marketing Strategy ('ABCDE')

- **Audience to be targeted -** By doing this, one can customise marketing efforts to make customers more likely to purchase and work on their needs, preferences, and pain points.

- **Branding** - Involves developing features (visual elements or personality) of a brand that help a consumer identify or associate with it. Including the company's branding elements across all marketing channels fosters brand recognition, establishes credibility, and builds trust with the target audience. This achieves long-term consistent success. An essential part of branding is understanding the organisation's vision and goals and incorporating them in a unique logo that portrays its core values. This marks potential customers' initial interactions with your products or services.

- **Competitive Analysis** - To differentiate your products or services from that of your competitors, highlight the additional benefits and features your products offer, so that customers prefer your offerings.

- **Define a multi-channel Marketing Plan** - This is a highly effective marketing approach for businesses. It involves utilising multiple channels such as social media, email, advertising, text messaging, and eCommerce to market your product. This way, customers can choose and subscribe to their preferred communication channels, helping you reach a wider audience.

- **Effectively measuring marketing success** - Marketing strategies necessitate continuous measurement and analysis to achieve a greater Return on Investment (ROI). Introduce key performance indicators (KPIs) such as website traffic, conversion rates, customer acquisition costs, and metrics to gauge the effectiveness of marketing campaigns.

Long-form content, Short-form video content and Chatbots

An effective marketing strategy often involves the use of long and short-form content.

Long-form content like blog posts, e-books, detailed videos, and podcasts can deliver value and in-depth information to the target audience while earning their trust.

Platforms like TikTok, Instagram reels, and YouTube 'Shorts' offer opportunities to craft captivating, visually attractive videos that grab the target audience's attention.

With the rise of AI, chatbots have become an increasingly prevalent trend in business marketing. These virtual assistants are developed to simulate human-like conversations and deliver personalised responses to user queries. Chatbots can seamlessly integrate into websites, messaging applications, or social media platforms. It increases customer interactions and offers 24/7 support, streamlining the overall customer experience.

Word-of-mouth Referral Marketing

Word-of-mouth (WOM) marketing involves an existing customer sharing a positive experience about a product with their peers.

Motivating customers to share their experiences involves delivering exceptional customer service alongside the product, ensuring a smooth ordering process, and consistently meeting delivery timelines.

Significant advantages of having WOM referral marketing include-

- **Credibility and trust** - Individuals tend to trust recommendations from familiar and respected sources more than traditional advertising approaches.
- **Cost-effectiveness** - It is a relatively low-cost form of promotion compared to traditional methods like TV, commercial print ads, or online display ads.
- **Amplified Reach and Targeting** - Targeted sharing by customers ensures that the information reaches individuals who are more likely to be interested in the product or service that is being recommended for people with similar interests.

Ethical Considerations in Marketing

Ethical marketing is a strategic approach in which businesses pledge to uphold open, transparent, responsible, and fair practices and to effectively communicate these values to their target market.

Critical Principles of Marketing Ethics

- **Fairness** - Establishing fairness as a decision-making principle means companies commit to fair practices, better wages, and sustainable development.
- **Honesty** - Honest companies use marketing communications to provide factual and unexaggerated information about their functionality and the impact of their products and services; they advertise without attempting to mislead.
- **Responsibility** - Businesses may emphasise their responsibility in several ways, including their obligation to provide a reliable product or service,

support social causes, give back to communities, treat their employees with respect, and protect the environment through sustainable practices.

- **Transparency**- In business, transparency means being open to the public about your company's operations, particularly the ethical way you treat employees and the sustainability and environmental impact of your products or services.

Ethical Marketing Examples

A charitable campaign - Donating money or goods to social causes and initiatives with a positive impact. The company donates one product to charity for every ten products it sells.

Centering business decisions and impact on product pages - Advertising the company's fair practices on product pages. The site may look inside the production process or provide accurate numbers about the product's minimal environmental impact. This aims to establish brand loyalty and make customers feel proud about supporting a company that works hard to be ethical.

Socially responsible social media accounts - Many companies work to show their ethical practices by being accountable and outspoken online about social and ethical issues. This marketing strategy emphasises that the company is an honest brand with a sense of social responsibility that customers want to support.

Marketing Mix

A Marketing mix refers to the tactics or marketing activities used to satisfy customers' needs and position your offerings clearly in the customer's mind.

Defining the marketing mix for a business involves using the '**7P marketing mix model**'. This model combines the traditional **4Ps,** which were used in marketing products or physical goods, and an additional **3Ps,** which help us meet the challenges of marketing services:

- Product, **P**lace, **P**rice, **P**romotion — **Products**
- **P**eople, **P**hysical evidence (Packaging), **P**rocess (Positioning)— **Services**

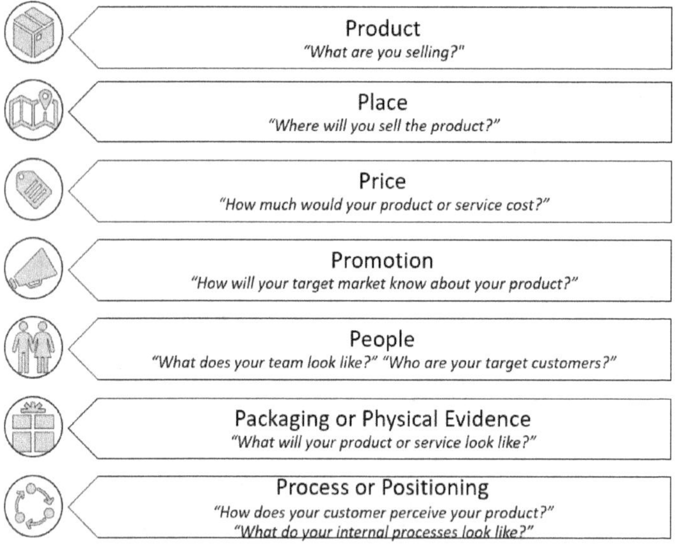

The 7P model offers a framework for a business to create a marketing plan, establish a unique selling proposition and effectively reach the target customers. It also serves as a guideline for a business to cover all of its bases regarding brand outreach.

While developing the 7P marketing mix, the business should consider how each element affects the rest, for example, how the price will affect the promotion strategy. This creates a unified brand experience for the customers.

Let's take a closer look at the 7Ps:

1. Product

"What are you selling?"

The Product sits at the centre of all marketing activities. Critically analysing the product is the key to marketing success. A Product can be physical goods, a service, or an idea created by an entrepreneur or an innovator to serve the customers' needs and address their existing problems.

To determine what problem your product solves, ask yourself questions such as these:

- Why is this product the best fit for my audience, and how would it benefit them?
- What would be the best design for the product?
- What variants would the product need to have to meet the needs of the target market?
- What quality of products is my audience seeking?
- Would the product be categorised as low/mid/high priced?
- How large is your target market?

Focus on creating a high-quality product or service, and with the right marketing strategy, it will eventually sell itself. In addition, knowing what the customers seek in a product will help you explain the value of your product to them. However, developing a product or service without identifying the target market is very risky and might lead to waste of resources and time.

2. Place

"Where will you sell the product?"

A place is the location or the area where the transactions are carried out. It also covers the product distribution and logistics. The 'place' should provide customers with a pleasant experience of buying the product or availing of the services so that they repeatedly visit (online or onsite). The place should be presentable, neat, and appealing to the target audience.

Here is a list of things to consider when choosing the right location:

- Where are people likely to look for your product - online or offline or both?
- Will people need to hold the product in their hands before buying?
- For physical stores - Is the location suitable for the target market? Is it likely to attract potential customers (Foot traffic)?
- Condition of the neighbourhood - What is the area's future potential concerning developments, laws, and regulations?
- Direct and indirect competitors
- Cost of doing business at this location

- Logistics - Do you own distribution channels? Or will you be working with partners to distribute your products? This will be important in determining the storage and transportation of products.
- How is the process of distribution of products or performance of service being done?
- Will you use storefronts?
- Would it be beneficial to talk to the customers directly as they browse your products (own website/store)? Or would it be good enough to have a third party interact with them (selling through third-party applications/ department store chains)?

3. Price

"How much would your product or service cost?"

Price is the value businesses assign to certain products or services after considering their cost, competition, objectives, Positioning, and the target market.

It is the only **P** in the **7Ps** that generates profit for the business, so this must be carefully done to establish a flow of revenue.

Following pricing guidelines must be followed to ensure a sustainable business:

- What is your product's perceived value, and how may your Pricing reflect this value? Are you looking to be perceived as a value-driven or premium brand?
- Use pricing strategies relevant to your market segment - How low can you go before the target

customer perceives it as 'low-quality', or conversely, how high can you go before they see you as 'overpriced'?

- Do not price the product or service below its cost price.
- Monitor competitors' pricing and ensure that your prices are at par with them unless your product or service is superior.
- Align prices with your business objectives.
- The product can be priced higher than the market to add value to your quality offering. It can also be at par with the demand to be competitive, offering more value in your offerings. Lastly, some companies initially tend to price their products lower to gain market share and then do a correction after establishing their product in the market.

4. Promotion

"How will your target market know about your product?"

Promotion involves presenting the products or services to the public and explaining how these can address the public's needs, wants, and problems.

Decide on the channels to reach your audience, like television and print advertising, display ads, stalls at product conferences, sales and discount promotion, social media marketing, email marketing, digital marketing (search engine optimisation, blogs, newsletters), or public relations.

Wherever competition is generally high, promotion is necessary for the Product's survival. Banks, IT, and consumer goods companies place themselves above the rest through advertising or promotions.

Some questions to consider:

- What marketing content will you publish for promotions and through which channels?
- Which marketing channels would reach the target market? Advertising helps raise awareness, while direct interactions with customers might build better relationships. If the target market is likely to be active on social media, that would be an effective strategy.
- Which advertising tools can be used to drive awareness and increase sales?
- At what time of the year is a customer likely to purchase your product? For example, a product that helps customers file their Income Tax returns would typically be used at the end of the financial year. Similarly, people tend to buy gold and gifts around festivals, so promotions for such products or services can be timed accordingly.
- How is the customer base responding to your promotion strategies? Spends can be adjusted accordingly.

Pay attention to the feedback from customers who have used your product/service and tailor promotional strategies suitably. For example, if people like your products but find them expensive, try to include what extra value they bring in future promotional activities.

5. People

"What does your team comprise?"

Today, people play a vital role in serving customers. With the influx of competitive products and services, one of the major differentiators is how the people of the business or employees make a difference in the customers' lives. This includes anyone who might come in contact with the customer, such as the product developers, marketing and sales teams, and customer service teams. While recruiting people, the roles and descriptions should be adequately identified so that they clearly know their purpose and serve the customers well.

Some points to consider are -

- What are the basic skills and qualifications needed for the job?
- What type of people are to be hired? Do they understand the brand personality? Do they know the product, and can they explain it to others?
- What leadership style will be applied by the entrepreneur?

Customer relationship management is critical to create a loyal customer base.

6. Packaging or Physical evidence

"What will your product or service look like?"

This is an essential element in the marketing mix for services.

For example, let us compare a restaurant with only chairs and tables and good food versus another one that also has ambient lighting, excellent music, suitable seating arrangements, and good nutritional food. Many customers will prefer the latter, where there is 'physical evidence' of the experience one can expect. In service marketing, physical evidence frequently stands out as a critical differentiator.

Consider a private hospital versus a government hospital. Typically, a private hospital boasts well-equipped doctor's offices, comfortable patient rooms, and efficient staff and is perceived to function seamlessly. A government hospital might lack some of these factors, and this becomes a differentiator.

In the case of products, this element would take the form of 'packaging'. A product's unique packaging may be an excellent way to catch your customer's attention when an array of similar products are in front of them. A well-designed package might also help customers identify your brand at a glance. For example, Nike shoes come in cardboard boxes with clean, symmetric lines and are well-known for displaying the iconic tick mark on a plain background.

7. Process or Positioning

"What internal processes will be followed by your company?"

"How is your product positioned in the current market?"

Process refers to how a service is delivered to the end customer- from pre-order interactions with the customer, placing the order, to delivering the order.

Companies like McDonald's and FedEx thrive on quick service because of their efficient internal processes.

The internal processes of a service company are of utmost importance to deliver consistent and good quality products. Hence, before establishing the service, the company should define precisely what processes to set up to ensure the customer's overall positive experience. Some points to consider are -

- How long does it take for the team to respond to customer queries?
- What happens once the customer orders - how does the internal team handle this, and what steps should they take?
- Are there enough staff members to cover busy times?
- How efficient are your scheduling and delivery logistics? Are you able to get the product to the customer on time?
- Optimising and documenting the company's processes (like use of ISO documentation guidelines) will give consistency and reduce human errors.

Respond quickly to customer complaints and use their feedback to improve your processes.

Positioning involves how the product is placed within the competitive market and in the customer's perception. How a customer 'perceives' your product is crucial for its success; for example, your product or service could be perceived as "more valuable but more expensive", "affordable but slightly lower quality", or "reliable". A business can carefully craft its positioning by highlighting its products' benefits, differences from the competitors, and unique products. Of course, the product needs to be able to deliver these promised benefits.

Examples of Marketing Mix

Amazon

Originating as an online bookstore, it swiftly diversified into selling music videos and other products. Rapidly, it became the world's largest online retailer, branching into industries from Cloud Computing to entertainment, becoming a significant player.

Amazon's Marketing Mix:

- **Product** - One-stop eCommerce stores offering a wide range of products.
- **Place** - Amazon is an internet-based retailer that ships to over 100 countries.
- **Price** - Products are affordable, with many items marked 20-25% lower than other stores, primarily because Amazon directly sources products from manufacturers.
- **Promotion** - Amazon employs a blend of conventional marketing channels such as TV and print ads alongside digital platforms like social media and PPC (Pay Per Click) ads. Additionally,

Amazon sponsors diverse events and makes substantial contributions to charitable causes.

- **People** - Anyone who needs to buy something from an online store is Amazon's target buyer.
- **Packaging** - Items purchased from Amazon arrive in a box featuring the brand's distinctive arrow markings on the side.
- **Positioning** - Amazon is a low-cost and convenient solution to people's shopping needs.

Google

A subsidiary of Alphabet Inc., Google is a technology company most commonly known for its search engine, which bears the same name. Google manages over 70% of global online search queries.

Google's Marketing Mix:

- **Product** - Products and services focus on search engine technology, AI, consumer products, and computer software. Products include Google (search engine), Pixel mobile devices, and Gmail.
- **Place** - Google runs its business on the internet. For physical products, retail stores are available in select countries.
- **Price** - The brand's pricing has different layers. Many of the services come with the 'Freemium' (business model where basic features are available to users at no cost but premium features are charged) pricing model. Google prices its physical products based on market demand, while its online

advertising services utilise a value-based pricing model.

- **Promotion** - Through advertisements across social media, print, television, and various digital platforms, Google enhances its product visibility. Additionally, Google sponsors events and collaborates with other businesses to extend the reach of its products.
- **People** - Anyone with an internet connection.
- **Packaging** - Google uses a sustainable, recyclable, plastic-free package to reduce its carbon footprint for physical products.
- **Positioning** - Google is positioned as one of the top search engines in the world, and helps people find relevant information on the internet based on keywords.

Nike

The world's most extensive sports footwear and apparel manufacturer and a major sports equipment manufacturer.

Nike's Marketing Mix:

- **Product** - Nike creates, produces, and markets athletic shoes, apparel, accessories, and sports equipment.
- **Place** - Customers can shop at Nike's online stores and retail outlets.
- **Price** - Uses a value-based and premium pricing system for its products.
- **Promotion** - Spends mainly on TV and social media ads. Their message - "Just do it" and "Do it against odds" fuels customers to achieve more

success. It also sponsors many sports teams and works with influential professional athletes.

- **People** - It primarily targets athletes or active people in physical fitness activities. They also have products for people who want to wear the latest trendy shoes.

- **Packaging** - Nike shoes and other products come in eco-friendly packaging made from recycled and recyclable cardboard materials, displaying the conspicuous tick on a plain orange background called the 'Swoosh' logo, representing motion and speed.

- **Positioning** - It has established its brand as the premier choice for professional athletes striving for the highest performance.

McDonald's

McDonald's is the world's leading Global foodservice retailer with over 37000 locations in over 100 countries. Over 90% of McDonald's restaurants are owned by independent local entrepreneurs.

- **Product** - McDonald's is a fast-food franchise offering a variety of items, including burgers, sandwiches, salads, and french fries.

- **Place** - McDonald's physical restaurants are on almost every continent, and most customers dine in or 'take away' from these outlets. Customers can also order their meals online.

- **Price** - The brand strives to maintain affordable pricing for its food items by keeping costs as low as possible.
- **Promotion** - McDonald's employs imaginative advertisements across TV, newspapers, billboards, and social media to maintain a prominent presence in people's minds. They also engage children through "Happy Meal" promotions, offering toys, sponsoring sporting events, and collaborating with celebrities.
- **People** - This includes enthusiasts of fast food, especially children, parents with young children and teenagers.
- **Packaging** - The packaging exudes a playful vibe, mirroring the happiness of dining at McDonald's. Much of the packaging material is sourced from recycled materials.
- **Positioning** – It is positioned as a "happy place" for individuals and families to spend quality time together. It also serves as a spot for a quick meal or socialising with friends.

In conclusion, the foundation of any marketing campaign lies in determining the five key elements of any marketing strategy ('ABCDE') along with the 7Ps of the Marketing Mix. The marketing mix delineates what a Brand must address to ensure its product's success in the market. Identifying the target audience is crucial for enhancing the impact of marketing endeavours. Businesses that can create the right marketing strategy to reach this audience and deliver upon customer needs and expectations will see the best results.

Chapter 2

BUILDING YOUR BRAND IDENTITY -CRAFTING A STRONG BUSINESS IMAGE

"Your brand is what other people say about you when you're not in the room." - **Jeff Bezos**

A 'brand' represents the qualities and reputation of a company and encompasses everything that defines the company, such as visual factors, personality, products, mission, values, and positioning. It is also connected to how people perceive the brand and the trust they develop over the years. The brand should deliver what it promises so that when people see the brand, they will see it as a reliable product or service.

Why is Branding important for a Business

Businesses create brands to differentiate themselves from their competitors. A top-quality brand will always attract customers and ensure continuous buying. Ultimately, a brand should enable a business to raise prices for its product or service without adversely affecting sales. A perfect example of this is **'Apple'**, which sells one of the most expensive phones in the market but remains popular due to its credibility and effective branding.

Brand Identity

Brand identity is crucial for ensuring that customers can easily identify and distinguish your brand. It includes the visual parts of a brand, like colours, designs, and logos, that allows people to remember and tell apart one brand from another. It also covers things like how a company's website looks, the packaging of its products, and what it posts on social media.

Why is Brand Identity crucial?

The different elements of the Brand Identity and the 'traits' of a brand (Brand Personality) give it a voice and uniqueness amid growing competition. It is necessary to keep the Identity consistent as this plays a pivotal role in marketing your products and services. In addition, having a good identity helps users associate products with the brand and makes it easy to recall.

Some examples of memorable Indian brands with significant Brand Identities:

- **Amul**

Amul is a dairy co-operative based in Gujarat. The company was founded in 1946 and is known for its high-quality dairy products like milk, butter, and cheese. Its brand identity is centred around the iconic 'Amul girl' in a Polka-Dot dress, which has become synonymous with the brand. The Amul Girl first appeared in an advertisement in 1967 and has become a cultural icon in India. Using the Amul girl in advertising and packaging has helped establish Amul as a trusted and reliable brand in the dairy industry.

- **Titan**

Titan is a watch and jewellery brand based in Bengaluru. The company was founded in 1984 and is known for its high-quality, reliable, stylish products. The Titan brand identity is built around the company's commitment to elegant design and innovation. The company's logo features an intelligent "T" in a distinctive font meant to represent the company's focus on elegance and sophistication. Using this logo across all of the company's products has helped establish Titan as a premium brand in the watch and jewellery industry.

• Paper Boat

Paper Boat is a beverage brand based in Bengaluru. The company was founded in 2016 and is known for its innovative and unique flavours. The Paper Boat brand identity is built around nostalgia and childhood memories. The company's packaging features colourful illustrations of childhood scenes, such as flying kites and playing hopscotch. Using these illustrations on the company's products has helped establish Paper Boat as a brand that values playfulness and creativity.

• Indigo

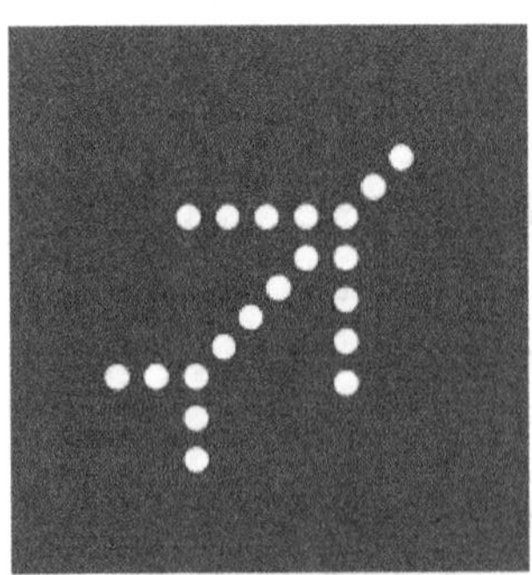

Indigo is an airline based in Gurugram. The company was founded in 2006 and is known for its low-cost and high-quality service. The Indigo brand identity is built around the company's commitment to affordability and efficiency. The company's logo is an image of a plane taking off, where the aircraft is made up of white dots. This logo symbolises freedom and movement, the desire for new horizons, and its core airline business. Using this logo across the company's branding and advertising has helped to establish Indigo as a low-cost career with a significant corporate image.

* **Vistara**

Vistara is a full-service airline based in Gurugram. The company was founded in 2013 and is known for its high-quality service and stylish cabin interiors. The Vistara brand identity is built around the concept of luxury and elegance. The company's logo features a stylised star in a distinctive font, which is meant to represent the company's focus on hospitality and comfort. Vistara is a premium airline brand in India.

- **Wildcraft**

Wildcraft is an outdoor gear brand based in Bengaluru. The company was founded in 1998 and is known for its high-quality and durable products. The Wildcraft brand identity is built around the concepts of adventure and exploration. The company's logo features a stylised mountain peak in a distinctive font (which also looks like a 'W'), representing the company's focus on outdoor adventure and travel. Wildcraft is a trusted and respected brand in the outdoor gear industry in India.

These are a few examples of Indian brands that have excelled in brand identity design. These brands display unique styles that set them apart from their competitors and have built successful customer loyalty. They have established strong connections with their target audiences by understanding their core values and telling compelling stories through their brand identity.

Brand Personality

Brand personality is when human traits and characteristics are linked to a brand, allowing customers to relate to it— essentially, giving a brand human-like qualities.

To simplify the concept even more, consider the following example.

Imagine how it would be if the company 'Apple' were human. Maybe it would be someone with an impeccable knowledge of languages, a perfect grasp of grammar, someone with excellent style, who maintains discipline even in demanding situations, and always chooses to wear premium quality clothes over regular ones.

That would be Apple's brand personality.

Why is Brand Personality influential?

Develops Brand Image – Brand identity and personality are intertwined tools that aid in crafting a desired brand image in the market. While brand personality shapes how a brand is perceived, brand identity brings this strategy to life visually. Together, they shape the brand's image.

Positions the Offering - Customers apply identical products from various brands in distinct ways. Brand personality instructs customers on the ideal usage of the brand's products. For example, **Nike** shoes are more reliable for sports because of their image of speed and power.

Develops an emotional connection - Like-minded people tend to build an emotional connection with a brand's personality. This helps the brand have more meaningful interactions and also helps with customer-powered marketing strategies like word-of-mouth marketing and loyalty marketing. For example, **Cadbury** brings out emotional connections between people in its ad series depicting "Kuch Meetha Ho Jaaye".

Eases Communication - Having a well-known personality endorse a brand makes it easier for the brand to communicate effectively with the customers. This is because the customers can link the personality traits of the famous individual with those of the brand. For example, Sachin Tendulkar was involved in advertisements for the beverage brand **Boost**, which helped users connect to their tagline of "Boost is the secret of my energy".

How to Build a Brand Personality

Brand personality is how the brand presents itself and behaves in front of customers. It includes tone, voice, associations, and all elements that set an individual apart and create an identity.

Developing a Brand Personality involves brand managers profoundly understanding their customers and crafting a personality that inspires the "like, know, and trust" factor. The intended audience should embrace, recognise, and trust this created personality.

It should:

- Attract the target audience by evoking a feeling of comfort, familiarity, and respect.
- Make the future target audience like the brand and appreciate and value the offerings.
- Repel the customers that the brand doesn't want to attract.

Dimensions of Brand Personality

The Journal of Marketing Research identifies five dimensions of brand personality: sincerity, excitement, competence, sophistication, and ruggedness [1]. The traits associated with these dimensions are detailed in the following figure:

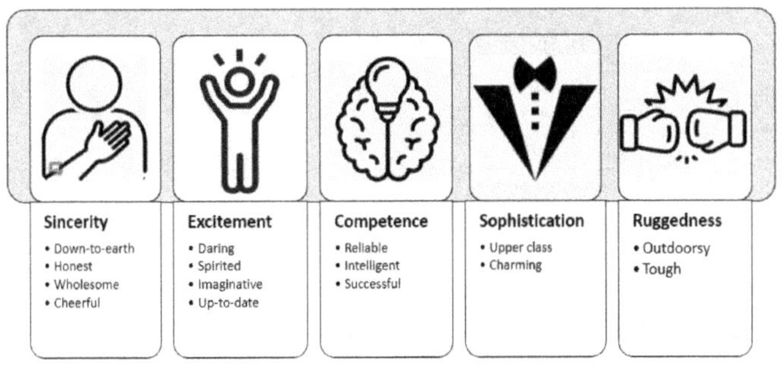

a

Examples of Brand Personality

- **Nike -** Nike has a brand personality that shows the **excitement** that athletes connect with. Their motto, "Just do it," embodies a determined, athletic individual chasing new goals. Nike often showcases vibrant colours like neon, giving off an energetic and youthful vibe in their products and marketing.

- **Amazon -** Amazon offers a personal relationship with its products and services, making it one of the most trusted and reliable brands globally. Its personality traits include **competence and sincerity**.

- **Coca-Cola -** Coca-Cola blends **excitement**, optimism and joy. Its special holiday packaging, brand colours, new flavours, and multiple campaigns, such as "Share a Coke", evoke a feeling of happiness, optimism, and innovation.

- **Apple** – Apple's focus is on <u>**sophistication and ruggedness**</u>. Apple's brand personality is about bringing lifestyle, innovation, and power to people through technology.

- **Google** - <u>**Competence**</u> is Google's brand personality. They aim to provide the best search results and continuously adjust them to ensure users find what they need.

- **McDonald's** - McDonald's personality can be <u>**excited**</u>, lighthearted, welcoming, and dependable.

- **Samsung** - Samsung's brand personality could be described as <u>**rugged and competent,**</u> as its products are seen as reliable, tough, and trend-setting.

Brand name and Tagline

The brand name and tagline are two of the most essential elements of your corporate branding strategy. They communicate your identity, value proposition, and personality in words to a target audience.

A tagline is a memorable phrase that embodies your business's core purpose and mission.

Examples of Taglines -

- Amazon - *Work hard, Have fun, Make history*
- Amul - *The Taste of India*
- Nike - *Just Do it*
- Apple - *Think different*
- Coca-Cola - *Taste the feeling*
- Big Bazaar - *Naye India ka Bazar*

- SBI- *Pure banking, Nothing else*
- Colgate- *Everyone deserves a future to smile about*
- Instagram- *Capture and share the world's Moments*
- Zomato - *Never have a bad meal*
- Flipkart - *Har wish Hogi Puri*
- Kit Kat - *Have a break, have a Kit Kat*
- YouTube- *Broadcast yourself*
- Samsung - *Do what you can't*
- Bank of Baroda - *India's International Bank*
- Citibank - *The Citi Never Sleeps*

Slogan Vs Tagline

Slogans are impactful phrases used in political, commercial, or religious contexts, often repeated, to communicate a specific idea or purpose to a targeted audience or group. They are crafted for marketing purposes, aiming for customer recognition and retention.

The goal is for consumers to remember the slogan and associate it with the product's benefits, making them choose that product when needed due to brand recall.

A comparison between Slogan and tagline:

Basis of Comparison	Slogan	Tagline
Meaning	A simple, straightforward, and memorable phrase used to advertise something	A brief and captivating phrase is used to convey a message to the public about the company.
Meant For	A product or ad campaign	The company itself
Flexibility	Flexible	Rigid
Appears in	Display ads, campaign packaging	Public-facing messages
Time Horizon	Short-Term	Long-Term
Objective	To demonstrate or validate the uniqueness of the company's product compared to its competitors.	To concisely convey the essence of the company's purpose or identity.

In conclusion, the company's marketing efforts primarily focus on capturing the audience's attention. Therefore, the brand's image, personality, tagline, and slogans hold significant importance and can be strategically leveraged by the firm to elicit the desired response from customers.

References:

[1] Jennifer L. Aaker, Dimensions of Brand Personality, Journal of Marketing Research, Vol. 34, No. 3 (Aug. 1997), pp. 347-356, American Marketing Association, http://www.jstor.org/stable/3151897

Chapter 3

TARGETING THE RIGHT AUDIENCE - IDENTIFY YOUR IDEAL CUSTOMERS

"There is only one winning strategy. It is to carefully define the target market and direct a superior offering to that target market." -
Philip Kotler

Have you ever seen an ad for a product or service and wondered who it was targeted at? Understanding the target audience for your marketing campaigns is crucial for creating suitable marketing material to attract the intended customers.

A target audience is a particular group most likely to purchase your product or service. Age, location, gender, interests, or income can dictate it.

Determining the target audience helps you create marketing content tailored to the right platform so that it resonates with them. Hence, this will help you get good returns for your marketing efforts and improve customer relations.

'Target audience' differs from your 'Target market' and 'Target Persona'.

Target Market	**Target Audience**	**Target Personas**
A broad group of people who **may be** interested in your product and services	Specific groups of people who are **most likely to buy** your products or services. Defines the target market using audience interests, demographics, or buying history.	**Ideal customer** to connect with, based on your target audience. It is a partly imagined portrayal of your perfect customer and mirrors the characteristics of the larger group it represents.
Broad	Specific	Personalized

Examples of Target Audiences

A. Business-Marketing platform
    a. Target Market: Small Businesses
    b. Target Audience:
        i. Local service-based business owners
        ii. Marketing managers for small e-commerce businesses
        iii. Freelance Marketing Consultants

B. Assisted Living Facility
    a. Target Market: Senior Citizens
    b. Target Audience:
        i. Seniors in a defined area
        ii. Working adults with senior parents in the specified area

C. Moving Company
    a. Target Market: People relocating to other places
    b. Target Audience:
        i. Urban apartment dwellers are likely to move more frequently
        ii. Suburban Families

How to find your target audience

To figure out the correct target audience, consider the following:

1. Start with your current customers

Look for demographics: What are the users' job titles, where do they live, and how old are they? Are there any patterns that emerge as you do so? Also, look for patterns with your local, loyal, and repeat customers. For B2B companies, this might include customer industry, number of employees, location, annual contract value, the revenue band of their purchases, and the profile of the employee making this purchase decision.

Talk to your customers: Get insights on why customers love your brand, product, and team. Also, identify where they spend their time and seek advice. Is it specific social media influencers, industry newsletters, or trusted company blogs? Using these questions when engaging with customers can assist in determining the most suitable marketing channels:

Questions about problems or pain points:

- What issue were you aiming to resolve?
- How were you addressing this issue before choosing our solution?
- Have you encountered any challenges with previous vendors?
- Were there any concerns about selecting our service?
- Are there areas where we can enhance our offering?

Questions related to Lifestyle/behaviour:

- How did you find out about us?
- What terms did you search for?
- What media or newsletter do you read related to this topic?
- What social media platform do you use?
- How much time do you spend online?

Questions related to your competitors:

- What made you choose us over our competitors?
- What is the primary benefit of the product or service?
- What additional benefits have you experienced?

- What do you like about us?

Once you have analysed the demographics and customer feedback, you can identify similar types of companies/people to market your product to. Compiling all the above information in a single place might be worthwhile to make the analysis easier.

2. Look at your social media followers

Your social media followers represent an established audience that provides insight into the demographic your current marketing resonates with. In addition, it gives you an idea of the consumers' profiles.

Consumers follow brands on social media:

a) To learn about new products.
b) To stay up to date on company news.
c) To learn about promotions or discounts.
d) To be entertained.
e) To be educated.

You can interact with your followers to find out what kind of content they like and which type responds well. Tailor your content to suit the platform; for example, Instagram has relatively younger users and more image-based content than Facebook, which has a slightly older audience and both textual and visual content.

3. Dig into your content analytics

The next type of audience you need to study is your website visitors:

a) Who is currently reading your content?
b) Who is downloading your articles?
c) Who is engaging with your videos?

Google Analytics, a service provided by Google, monitors and presents data on website traffic, mobile app traffic, and related events. This will help you learn the following:

a) Demographics: User breakdown by location, city, and country
b) Where are users coming from?
   - Is a particular social media platform a significant referral source?
   - Is it a niche industry (having a high-end product) or a new site (a green-field industry with newly added users)?
   - Is it through a particular blog?

   This information will assist in determining where to target your marketing campaigns. Understanding the topics that engage or don't engage your website visitors can offer insights into your target audience and guide strategies to better appeal to them.

c) Which terms are they using in their search?

In short, find out what users look up in search engines (like Google), leading them to your site.

4. Participate in Exhibitions and Conferences

Another way to identify your target audience and gain new customers, especially in B2B businesses, is to participate in exhibitions or product conferences. In this case, your target audience will be those who visit, interact with, and learn from your exhibit. You can collect your visitors' business cards and ask them to complete a questionnaire on their desired product details. This way, you will have confirmed customer leads. These exhibitions and conferences are also helpful to gain information on the product portfolios of your competitors.

5. Check out your competitors

Examine your competitors' marketing focus:

a) Where do they advertise? Who are they targeting with their ads?

b) What pain points are they addressing? Analyse and see how they compare with yours, including how they overlap and differ.

6. Set your parameters

It is important to identify who your customer isn't. This can be done by analysing customer interviews, social media following, website visitors, and competitor audiences.

By doing so, you can identify the gaps in your customer base. For example, if your product serves only Indian customers, your target audience does not include anyone operating outside these boundaries.

Establishing your parameters will help steer both your marketing and business strategy.

How to connect with your target audience

According to the target audience's preferences, these tools can be utilised to engage with them:

- **Email**– You can send a detailed newsletter that targets a particular group of people, nurture email flows that target leads, and trigger emails at current customers.
- **Event** – You can host an event for the entire community or one that caters to potential customers, current customers, or prospective partners.
- **Community** – Consider forming a group that connects potential customers with similar roles or a community that unites all users of the product.

- **Social media account for the business** - Consider creating and sharing a thought leadership article aimed at influencers for potential sharing, a promotional video customised for potential customers, or hosting an interview series featuring noteworthy figures like authors, celebrities, or experts relevant to your audience.

- **Ads** - Social media ads help introduce your products to your target audience and provide insights into their preferences.

  On **Facebook**, three types of people can be targeted with ads-

  a. **Core Audience** - Base market segment. This will help you build a baseline for your audience using parameters like Location, Demographics, Interests, Behaviour, and Connections of your Target users.

     For example, people in cold weather regions might find an ad on 'winter coats' proper. People with anniversaries coming up might be interested in ads for gifts. People interested in sports might want to purchase team jerseys. Offering free samples or discounts might help you convert the ad viewer to a customer.

  b. **Custom Audiences** – These groups are individuals who already have some awareness about your brand. The primary data sources for your custom audiences are Contact lists (existing customers who are part of the platform) and Site visitors (target people who have visited your websites). Reminding users of the products they visited previously might nudge them to go ahead with the purchase.

c. **Lookalike Audiences** -These are segments of people who have similar characteristics to your existing audience and are likely to be interested in similar ads.

Google Ads - This platform facilitates reaching individuals actively seeking what your business offers. Through continuous improvements, it guides explicitly those interested in your products or services to your website.

Instagram Ads - Businesses can craft new ads featuring product tags or enhance their existing shopping posts within the Instagram app to expand the audience for their shoppable content.

In conclusion, define and leverage your target audience to formulate a focused marketing strategy. Analyse the profiles of your current and prospective customers across various platforms to understand the demographics interested in your product or service. Additionally, checking out your competitors' target audience and marketing content may help you tweak your marketing strategy.

Continuously updating your target audience helps you accurately understand your user base. While identifying your target audience is crucial, it's not the ultimate step. For effective marketing, everyone on your team must embrace these customer profiles. Once defined, widely share them to ensure all your business communications resonate with the most important ones.

Chapter 4

CAPTIVATING YOUR AUDIENCE - CREATING COMPELLING CONTENT STRATEGIES

"Content marketing is more than a buzzword. It is the hottest trend in marketing because it is the biggest gap between what buyers want and what brands produce." – **Michael Brenner**

Content marketing strategically focuses on crafting and circulating valuable, pertinent, consistent content to captivate and retain a precisely defined audience, aiming to prompt profitable customer engagement. The right content marketing plan should attract and engage your target audience while driving business goals. Such a strategy establishes expertise, promotes brand awareness, and boosts loyalty and trust.

You can generate content in various formats, such as blogs, newsletters, surveys, tool reviews, e-books, social media posts, quizzes, video giveaways, podcasts, or user-generated content.

The 5 Cs of Content Creation

The content must talk directly to the customer and should have "magic words" that have a powerful, direct impact on sales. Including words like 'free', 'you', 'discover', 'amazing', 'guaranteed', 'act now' or 'save' in your marketing content may urge the user to take the expected action.

1) **Be Consistent** - If you already have a presence on Twitter, Facebook, and LinkedIn, posting business blogs solely to your website is redundant. However, featuring one or two blogs per week will help attract a broad target market and maintain their interest in your brand.

2) **Be Contextual** – Customise your content to resonate with your specific buyer persona. Consider the times when your target market is likely to consume your content – whether it's in the mornings before going to work, during lunch breaks, evenings, or weekends, which will attract a broader audience.

3) **Be Cohesive-** Ensure that your content marketing remains cohesive by aligning the content across all marketing platforms with one primary strategy. Use

the same information, logos, and fonts on every platform, as this will help to avoid confusion amongst your audience and enable them to identify your brand immediately.

4) **Be Concise -** To ensure your post has a broad reach, create short, engaging, and simple content that conveys the main point.

5) **Be Credible -** If you include information in your content taken from other sources, be sure to quote the source. Always write honestly and transparently and follow ethical practices.

Types of Content

Here are a few of the types of content your brand can create -

1. **Blog posts**: Published as a website and offer valuable information for your audience that establishes your expertise on a subject. It also helps to build brand awareness, as users' search terms might find 'hits' on your blog and lead them to helpful content.

2. **E-books:** Lead-generation tools that attract people to a website. They are typically longer and more in-depth than a blog. Often, websites allow visitors to download e-books after entering their contact information, producing a direct lead for the sales team.

3. **Case studies**: This allows you to talk about a real-life scenario where your product was used by a

customer, which not only highlights the uses of your product but also serves as a positive review for it.

4. **Infographics**: A combination of visual elements and words may sometimes be more effective in engaging with an audience than words alone. They are also easily shareable, as they are usually smaller in size compared to, say, blogs. You can also include branding elements like your logo, increasing brand visibility.

5. **Emails**: Newsletters and email lists enable you to regularly appear in your users' email inboxes, offering opportunities to remind your customers of your brand while providing valuable information and updates about your products.

6. **Testimonials and reviews**: Created by compiling user-provided data and are great at increasing your products' reliability factor.

7. **Videos**: Highly engaging content and shareable across social media and websites. It requires more time/resource investment than the above forms of content but has good returns on investment.

8. **Podcasts**: Useful when your audience does not have time to read content, but just like videos, it takes time to create and edit them.

9. **Social media**: This is a valuable way to reach your target audience, as most people frequently use social media. You can repurpose content from your blogs

into new formats and share it across multiple platforms.

How to Create a Content Marketing Strategy

A content marketing strategy delineates the purpose behind creating content, the intended audience, the nature of the content and the distribution approach.

1. **Define a goal:** Why do you want to produce content? What business goals do you want to achieve by doing so? The primary aim is to demonstrate how your product or service effectively resolves customer issues. For example, if it is customer retention, you might want to post about troubleshooting techniques or 'How-to' videos for a product or highlight the different ways they can use it alternatively if the aim is to establish credibility as an expert in a particular field. However, if the objective is to demonstrate expertise in a specific subject area, you could publish more studies on relevant topics in your field

that might lead the consumer to believe your products are reliable.

2. **Use your buyer persona** to create content relevant and specific to them. As you learn more information about your users, use it to fine-tune your content.

3. **Audit your content**: Run a content audit across all your platforms to check which types of content are performing the best and which are the worst, as well as their relevance and quality, which, in turn, help you determine which topics are most beneficial to your customers, find gaps in the content topics, and develop new ideas for future content.

4. **Find out how to reach your target audience:** Do they reach out through your blogs, email inquiries about your products, or connect via social media? Tailor your content accordingly and increase sharing frequency on these platforms to better engage with your audience.

5. **Publish regularly:** Once you understand your audience and the best content formats, create a short plan (3-6 months) to list which type of content you need ready by when.

Content Marketing Examples

- **Amul Dairy Co-operative Society:** You must have seen Amul's iconic Polka Dot Girl on the covers of all Amul dairy products. Amul also uses her in their marketing content, together with a caption, which is usually a pun on some current affairs item. They post their content in newspapers and on social media and have a high number of followers on each of these platforms.

Amul is an ideal example of content that reflects current affairs.

- **Flipkart**: Flipkart, a prominent Indian e-commerce platform, offers a wide array of products, including home appliances, electronics, groceries, and clothing. Recognized for top-tier content marketing, their ads and social media content resonate with customer sentiments while also highlighting their website's features. Their recent "India ka fashion capital" tagline in celebrity-driven commercials effectively raised public awareness about their latest trends and promotions.

Flipkart exemplifies how content marketing shapes the public's perception of a brand.

- **Shaadi.com**: Most of their ads revolve around female-centric themes, recognizing that marriage decisions often pose a more significant challenge and commitment for girls. In their recent advertisement, a mother acknowledges her daughter's refusal of an unwanted marriage proposal. Shaadi.com effectively connects with its audience by acknowledging this societal context. Moreover, their ads feature the application's interface, showcasing characters effortlessly navigating profiles and features. Shaadi.com maintains a consistent presence in ads and on YouTube.

It is a great marketing example of customer-centric content.

- **Swiggy**: Swiggy's content revolves around posting pictures of mouth-watering food options, playful tweets, and trending hashtags to engage customers. Additionally, on social media, short videos highlight Swiggy's swift delivery and showcase enticing offers to captivate the audience's attention. For example, customers could avail of up to a 60% discount on food orders for six minutes after every six scored during the cricket match. They brought this to the consumer's attention by displaying videos and ads on their YouTube channel and TV.

  Swiggy is an example of a brand with engaging content.

- **Vodafone India Limited:** Unlike traditional ad templates used by other cellular providers, Vodafone ads convey messages through minimal or no speech. Their famed 'Zoo Zoos' ads, featuring amusing characters in typical scenarios, effectively introduced customers to offers, plans, and recharge options. These visuals resonated with the public, transcending language and cultural differences by prioritising visuals over audio for message delivery.

  It is an exemplary content marketing instance, breaking language barriers and uniting people nationwide.

- **Pizza Hut India**: Pizza Hut is that one-weekend hangout spot where we all plan to treat ourselves to delicious pizzas with our friends. They offer several 1 + 1 pizzas ("Buy one, get one free") and combo offers that make for an ideal weekend brunch. Their pizzas come in various flavours and toppings, with vegetarian and non-vegetarian options. With a physical footprint across multiple cities, the surge in online orders has emphasised the importance of a robust social media presence and active content marketing. Their engaging posts prompt viewers to tag friends, share comments, or share Pizza Hut memories for a chance to win complimentary pizzas and exclusive offers.

It is a great content marketing example to engage with the audience and create awareness among more people.

- **Cafe Coffee Day:** Cafe Coffee Day (CCD) is an Indian coffee retail chain renowned for brewing cups of coffee domestically and internationally. CCD's coffee outlets are renowned for their lavish interiors, providing the perfect ambiance for business discussions or relaxation before your next journey. On their social media accounts, they greet you with new, delicious-looking bakery and coffee options. Recently, CCD also held events for consumers' pets on National Puppy Day. They sent out invites to pet owners and their pets to celebrate the occasion.

Another example of content marketing is Cafe Coffee Day, created after understanding customers' preferences.

- **Vicks:** This pharmaceutical firm produces tablets, vapour rubs, and inhalers. Renowned for their products aimed at alleviating coughs and decongesting stuffy noses, their impactful advertising campaign showcased children and adults benefiting from the healing properties of their VapoRubs. Also, their TV and YouTube ads feature a famous cricketer using a Vicks tablet ("Vicks ki Goli") to heal his sore throat ("Khich Khich"). Vicks is also present on Twitter, Instagram, and Facebook. "Khich Khich" expression is also used to depict current affairs and humour in their posts.

Vicks sets an exemplary standard in content marketing by seamlessly blending product-centric information with creative and quirky social media posts and incorporating influencers to enhance their content strategy.

These are some of the most compelling content marketing strategies used by brands in India. From emotional appeal to engaging content, these brands have successfully leveraged the power of content marketing and continue to regenerate results by creating qualitative, interactive, and relevant content. Some brands also spend money on agencies, who then help them craft the ideal content to increase brand awareness and generate leads.

As mobile data expenses decrease in India, companies have a wider reach across diverse demographics and regions for content marketing and services.

Chapter 5

LEVERAGING SOCIAL MEDIA AND WEBSITES - ONLINE PRESENCE MASTERY

"Social media is about sociology and psychology more than technology." - **Brian Solis**

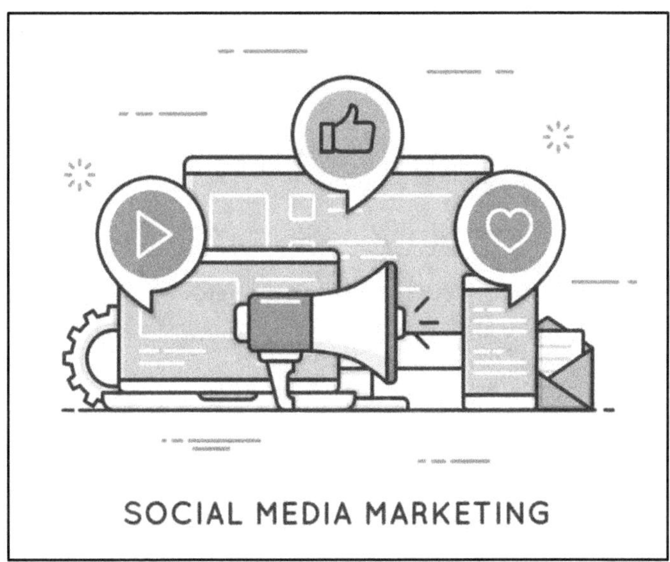

In the current era of online shopping, it is essential for businesses to maintain a strong digital presence. Social Media Marketing (SMM) harnesses the influence of popular platforms like Facebook, Instagram, Twitter, or LinkedIn to promote brands, expand target audiences, boost website visits, and drive sales.

SMM requires an evolving strategy with measurable goals and includes:

a) Maintaining and optimising your profile by providing accurate website links and having working Call-To-Action (CTA) buttons. A 'CTA' button is a prompt on a website that tells the user to take a specific action, such as 'Sign Up', 'Buy Now' or 'Donate'.
b) Posting pictures, live videos, or stories (temporary multimedia content) that represent your brand and attract relevant audiences.
c) Managing responses to comments, shares, and likes while overseeing your reputation.
d) Cultivating relationships with followers, customers, and influencers to foster a thriving brand community.
e) Paid advertising through social media to reach targeted audiences.

Benefits of Social Media Marketing

Due to its extensive reach and adaptability, social media is one of the most effective free marketing channels for businesses today.

Here are some advantages of SMM:

- **Facilitates quicker and simpler content distribution** - Social media empowers your business to actively engage with your market. Your profile, posts, and interactions with users help create a relatable persona that your audience can connect with and trust.

- **Provides a cost-effective marketing platform -** Due to their extensive reach, businesses can set up free profiles on social media platforms, making them excellent product promotion tools.

- **Boosts website traffic** - Among profile links, blog post shares, and advertisements, social media is a primary channel for boosting website traffic and converting visitors into customers.

- **Enables regular interaction with the Target audience** - You can directly create leads and conversions with your target audience on these platforms using features such as Instagram or Facebook shops, direct messaging, profile Call to Action buttons, and appointment booking features.

- **Increases brand awareness** - Social media's visual nature enables you to craft a strong visual identity across broad audiences, enhancing brand awareness and yielding excellent mileage for marketing campaigns.

- **Gives a complete insight into the industry marketplace** - Social media enables you to monitor your customer satisfaction, stay updated on the latest industry trends, and track your competitor's activities.

Larger and actively engaged audiences on social media networks simplify the attainment of your marketing objectives.

Social media marketing statistics [1]

1. The number of internet users in India has grown to **692 million** (48.7 percent of India's total population).

2. The number of social media users is **467 million** owing to widespread internet connectivity among people.
3. Indians, on average, spend about **2.36 hours** on social media daily (in 2023). Social media has become one of India's most essential parts of daily internet usage.

Total Population of India	1.42 billion
Number of Internet users	0.692 billion
Number of mobile internet users	0.627 billion
Active social media users	0.467 billion
Average daily time spent using the internet	6.23 hrs
Average daily time spent using social media	2.36 hrs

4. Falling smartphone prices have driven a massive increase in the usage of mobile smartphones across India.
5. The easy availability of super-fast internet at low prices has also increased social media usage.
6. The usage of apps like YouTube and WhatsApp has increased due to the increased prevalence of fast internet connectivity.

Critical Elements for a Flourishing Social Media Marketing Strategy

A successful SMM strategy will look different for every business and platform, but here are things they will all have in common:

a) Knowledge of your audience

To engage your target audience, it may be helpful to understand:

- What platforms they use
- When they use the platform
- What kind of content they like
- Who else they are following
- What they are talking about amongst their peers, and how they converse (ensuring your content 'speaks' the same language)

b) Brand identity

What message do you aim to communicate to your audience? What emotions do you seek to evoke regarding your brand when they engage with your content?

c) Content strategy

Though spontaneity is present on social media, a structured content strategy is vital for upholding a consistent voice and consistently delivering high-quality content.

Quantifiable insights will help you prepare your strategy, including who you are reaching, the right content to share, and the best times to post.

d) Regular activity

Social media operates in real time. To leverage it for business growth, regular posting, active engagement, responsiveness to interactions, staying abreast of trends, and maintaining an updated profile are crucial.

e) In-bound approach

Avoid using social media solely for business pitches. Instead, prioritise offering value through engaging and informative content while cultivating a community around your business. This approach naturally promotes your brand; eventually, your audience may advocate for it by sharing your content.

Critical Steps for a Successful Social Media Marketing Strategy

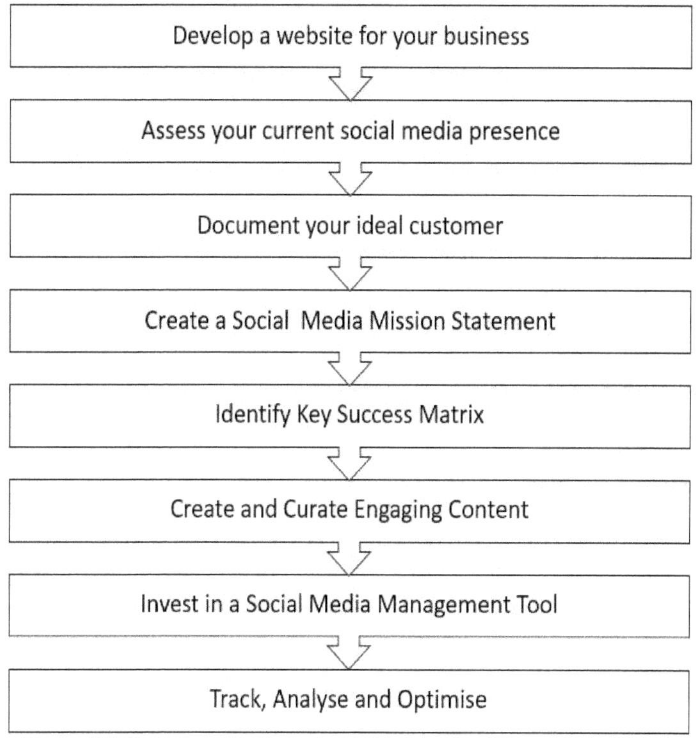

Step 1 – Develop a website for your business

Design a website keeping in mind your brand identity and personality. Here, you can give detailed information about your product portfolio, team, customer reviews, links to social media accounts, and contact information. This website can be mentioned on your social media accounts too. Having all this information in one place is also helpful while pitching your business to potential financial investors. The contact information section is significant, and you should promptly respond to customer inquiries.

Step 2 - Assess your current social media presence

Following areas to consider when auditing your business's social media presence

a) Which networks are you currently active on?
b) Have you optimised your networks? Adding a profile photo, page cover images, a short Bio, or including your website link can help more people discover you.
c) Which networks currently provide the most value?
d) How do your profiles stack up against your competitors' profiles?

If you are newly building your online presence, skip this step.

Step 3 – Document your ideal customer

Use the factors listed below to create a highly focused buyer persona:

- Age
- Location
- Job title
- Income
- Pain points (that your business can solve)
- Frequently used social network(s)

You could create a tailored campaign based on the above points, making them more effective and helping you gain the right social media followers and eventual customers.

Step 4 – Create a Social Media Mission Statement

Craft a precise social media mission statement outlining your intentions for utilising your social presence, aligning with your brand identity. This statement will guide your future strategies, hence you should consider your ideal customer when formulating it.

Some examples -

- **Facebook** - "Give people the capacity to form communities and bring the globe closer together."
- **Amazon** - "To be Earth's most customer-centric company."
- **WhatsApp** - "We desire to let people communicate anywhere in the world without barriers."
- **YouTube** - "To give everyone a voice and show them the world."
- **Twitter -** "To empower everyone to create and share ideas and information instantly without any limitations.

Step 5 – Identify Key Success Matrix

How do you plan to measure the success of your social media marketing, not just in acquiring more followers but also in generating revenue and enhancing the bottom line? A few metrics to consider measuring are:

- Conversion rate (how fast a visitor becomes a customer)
- Time spent on the website
- Reach (how big is your community, how many people are viewing your content)
- Brand mentions (how many people are saying your brand in their social media posts)
- Sentiment (how is your brand being perceived)
- Total shares (how many times has your content been shared)

Step 6 – Create and Curate Engaging Content

You know your ideal customer, so you can use that information to create a social media mission statement. With this, it should be easy to begin creating and curating content tailored to suit the platform of your choice.

Consider creating various types of contents such as images, videos, blog posts, company news, infographics, eBooks, and Interviews. Content drives social media, so prioritise crafting high-quality, engaging content. Developing a 'content calendar' can help in:

- Determining posting frequency for each network
- Identifying topics to discuss or share
- Scheduling the timing for sharing them

This way, you have a regular schedule for the content that needs to be posted. One point to note is that the 'voice' and 'tone' of your content should suit both the target audience and the platform.

Step 7 - Invest in a Social Media Management Tool

Having a presence across multiple social platforms is very useful. Still, managing all of them at once can get challenging - regular content posting, replying to customers' inquiries, and finding new customers. Hence, using a social management tool to scale your efforts quickly might be beneficial. One of the benefits of such a tool is the ability to schedule posts ahead of time. Ensure alignment with the content calendar created earlier.

Step 8 – Track, Analyse and Optimise

Predicting the most effective platform for your business is challenging. Therefore, tracking social media statistics, analysing the data, and adjusting accordingly can be highly beneficial. Each previous step should be reevaluated occasionally to ensure we direct all marketing efforts correctly. For instance, if you discover that Facebook or Twitter is your most impactful channel after a few months of content sharing, contemplate amplifying your efforts on those platforms.

The Best Current Social Media Platforms for Business

a) **Facebook**

It is the largest global social media platform and one of the most extensive local business directories.

- It is accessible from any device with an active internet connection.
- You may post text, pictures, and multimedia and share them with other users and friends.
- Brands use Facebook to host events, sell products, announce their product line, create an account around them, and perform various other functions.
- People of all age groups use it to communicate with friends and family.

b) **YouTube**

It is a free video-sharing website that makes it easy to watch online videos.

- You can upload videos to your channel, share, leave comments, and show appreciation by 'liking' other videos.
- Customers can follow or subscribe to your channel to get updates.
- You can curate videos relevant to your product, compile them, and post them on your channel. By providing a clear description and including the right hashtags, your video may show up as a 'suggestion' to users looking for products similar to yours or search terms matching the video's description.
- Most of the other video-sharing platforms can host only short videos, so businesses can add their longer videos to YouTube and add the link to other platforms.

- Useful for marketing as people use it as a 'search engine' for videos
- Allows users to create ads
- Target audience - Primarily millennials, but used by a diverse audience across locations, genders, and ages.

c) Instagram

It is a popular photo and short video-sharing platform that has also become popular as a mode of communication between brands and individuals.

- You have the option to share pictures, stories (temporary multimedia content), and reels (short videos) on this platform. You can also combine multiple photos and videos as 'Reels'.
- You can geotag images with location names.
- It is widespread, especially among influencers who use the app to make a living.
- You can set up your 'shop' on this platform, allowing users to discover and browse products and include CTA buttons for buying them.
- You can also create posts as paid ads.
- Target audience - Primarily millennials

d) LinkedIn

It is a professional network that celebrates leadership, learning, and core business values used for the following:

- White-collar networking, job prospects, and professional development
- Job hunters can upload their resumes, and employers can post jobs
- Helps to build an industry-specific network
- Can include links to external websites and blogs as part of posts.

- Sharing company milestones and culture
- Post industry news and insights
- Target audience - People in white-collar jobs

e) Twitter

It is a beautifully tangled network of quick thoughts, useful tidbits, and energised discussions.

- Twitter posts are primarily text-based. Users post and interact using "Tweets", messages with a 280-character limit.
- The platform allows registered users to post, like, or retweet tweets, while unregistered users may only read public tweets.
- People can follow each other to get updates regarding their posts and keep up with news and trends.
- Allows companies to provide quick customer service and support by 'replying' to customer tweets or 'DMs' (Direct Messages in the Inbox)
- Allows users to post-paid ads.
- Target audience - It is popular among all age groups.

f) Snapchat

You can build an audience with fun images and short videos as they focus locally.

- Content includes photos, videos, and text messages, which are visible only for a short period of time (24 hours).
- Peer-to-peer photo sharing and stories;
- A "Discover" feature lets brands show short-form content supported by ads.
- Target audience - Primarily Gen Z, followed by Millennials

g) Tik Tok

Share videos for entertainment.

- More famous for dancing, funny or inspiring videos
- It is also renowned for participating in trending challenges.
- Target audience - Primarily Gen Z

h) WhatsApp

It is the most popular messaging platform in India.

- Primarily text-based messages, but also allows the attachment of multimedia.
- Intuitive and straightforward User Interface (UI) makes it easy for users to learn how to use the application.
- It helps businesses keep in touch with customers and update them on new products and promotional activities. It also allows companies to 'broadcast' common messages to user lists.
- It is also helpful for customer support as the customer can directly chat with the business and resolve complaints/queries.
- WhatsApp is available internationally and supports cross-country communication via the Internet.
- Target audience - Diverse across all age groups.

i) Telegram

It is a globally available multi-platform, cloud-based instant messaging application.

- Posts include encrypted chats, video calling, and file sharing.

- Share unlimited images, documents, locations, audio files and stickers, text and voice messages, and video calls.

j) Moj

Released after the ban of TikTok in India.

- Used to create short videos with exceptional effects
- The application supports 15 languages
- Target audience - Primarily Gen Z

k) ShareChat

Leading Indian social media platform that allows users to share their opinions, document their lives, and make new friends in their native language.

Summary of social media apps and their uses

	Primary content	Primary Audience	Salient features
Facebook	Text, Multimedia	Millennials and older	Can host Live events; Sell products; Allows external links; Has a broad reach; Allows long videos; Targeted ads
YouTube	Long-form videos	Diverse	One of the few apps to allow long-form video content; Has a broad reach; Targeted ads

Instagram	Photos, Short-form videos	Millennials and younger	Appealing interface; Editing tools for posts; Can host Live events, sell products via 'Shop'; Has a broad reach; Targeted ads.
LinkedIn	Text, Multimedia	White-collared professionals	Industry-specific marketing/networking, Allows external links; Can host Live events; Has a broad reach in professional circles.
Twitter	Short-form text	Diverse	Accessible to 'Tweet' and get replies; Provide short updates; Good for customer support.
Snapchat	Short-form videos	Gen-Z	Quirky content which lasts for only 24 hours; Editing tools for posts; Useful to reach a younger audience
Tik Tok	Short-form videos	Gen-Z, Millennials	Useful to reach a younger audience; Has a broad reach in some locations; Targeted ads.

WhatsApp	Text, Multimedia	Diverse	Easy UI; Quick personal or group replies; Good for Customer Support; Has a broad reach
Moj	Short-form videos	Gen-Z	Useful to reach a younger audience; Limited reach
ShareChat	Text with native language support	Across age groups	Supports 15 local languages; Limited reach
Telegram	Text, Multimedia	Diverse	Easy UI; Useful for customer support; Limited reach

Pros and Cons of Employing Social Media Apps for Businesses

Pros	Cons
Low cost	Content creation and management require dedicated resources.
Easy to share content	Privacy concerns for consumer photos/ videos, Spam connections
Huge customer base	Misinformation concerns regarding the validity of data; Ensuring content is accurate
Enables posting various content types	Security concerns - Hackers; Conduct a regular audit of all

with attractive formatting options	accounts
Targeted advertising, also connected to Google searches	Negative feedback visible to everyone - Must be addressed immediately
Can host Live events	Some apps have text limitations (Twitter, 240 characters) or video length limitations (Instagram, 60 seconds)
Easy for the brand to be 'found' by customers	Some apps require your contact number (WhatsApp, Telegram)
Almost all of them have free membership (some have a paid premium subscription)	Many apps have complex algorithms that decide which content users view, which might be challenging to understand

Establishing a digital footprint, mainly via social media, proves highly effective in marketing your range of products. Regardless of your platforms or strategies, the crucial point is that social media isn't a platform for direct business pitches. It is a place to build a community, express your brand personality, demonstrate your values, and share helpful information. With the right content, businesses can widen their consumer base, multiply and increase profits.

Reference- [1] https://www.theglobalstatistics.com/india-social-media-statistics/

Chapter 6

LEVERAGING EMAIL MARKETING - UNLOCK THE POWER OF DIRECT COMMUNICATION

"Email has an ability many channels don't: creating valuable, personal touches - at scale." - **David Newman**

Email marketing is a powerful tool that captures the attention of users by sending targeted emails to subscribers. It serves to educate, entertain, answers, and provide valuable information to readers, keeping them connected to the business. It is one of the best marketing tools influencing customers' buying habits. Running an email marketing campaign keeps you in touch with your customers. A business that stays in touch with its customers stays in business for a long time.

Strategies for a thriving email marketing campaign

a) Identify your goals

First, establish the aim of the email campaign. Is it:

- i) Boosting your sales?
- ii) Developing a personal relationship with your customers?
- iii) Capturing people's attention?
- iv) Focusing on improving customer experience?

b) Gain engagement with your content

To increase the interaction of users with your posts, you could:

- i) Create an active blog where unique content is published regularly.
- ii) Send notifications to your customers regularly through emails informing them about the recently added content and product updates.
- iii) Encourage subscribers to share the content with friends on social media by offering them sops.

c) Personalise Every Email

Emails that begin with the generic Dear Sir /Ma'am put off your reader. It shows that not much thought has gone into sending those emails. Always add your subscribers' names while addressing them.

d) Use Captivating Images

No one likes to read a plain chunk of boring text. Include some colourful images that reflect your brand identity and personality. Include text in large fonts inside your pictures, as people will most likely read them.

e) Optimise for Multiple Devices

Ensure you design emails responsively, catering to mobiles, tablets, and desktops for optimal viewing. To optimise it for mobile, create content with a great subject line below 50 characters.

f) Include a Meaningful CTA (call to action)

Every email must have a point to it. Otherwise, you take up your subscriber's valuable time and inbox space. It is essential to wrap up every email with an appropriate Call-to-Action button, for example, 'Buy Now', 'Learn More', or 'Watch this video now'.

g) Use a comprehensive email builder

An HTML email builder can help build a successful email marketing campaign. Email builders can help you create, optimise, and personalise your emails by dragging/dropping elements to make an email that reflects your brand personality while creating uniquely presented information.

h) A/B test your Emails

It is known as split testing. A marketing experiment involves segmenting your audience to test different variations within a campaign and assess their performance. It means displaying version A of marketing content to one segment of your audience and version B to another segment to determine the more practical option.

Top Email Marketing Tools in India [1]

a) **OCTANE.in** - Founded on the idea that each email marketing campaign can achieve intended outcomes with appropriate tools. Combining integrated marketing, performance marketing, and permission marketing alongside agile marketing technology and expert service makes it a compelling choice.

b) **Mail Marketer** - A reputable do-it-yourself digital marketing agency that manages email campaigns. Mail Marketer excels at delivering mass emails, promotions, event invites, newsletters, and bulk emails. With Mail Marketer, you can pick up a plan. Sign up and automate your campaign without installing the software or establishing mail servers. It can fit into any budget, whether a small-list business or one that needs to send millions of emails.

c) **MailGet Bolt** - Assists in sending bulk emails without the need for hosting or a different SMTP (Simple Mail Transfer Protocol) configuration. You may send emails using its SMTP and the link to other SMTP services like Amazon SES, Mail Gun, Mandrill, and SendGrid. The drag-and-drop email builder, autoresponders, drips, and list management are among its standard features, facilitating swift email creation. Deliver emails automatically based on a preset schedule to engage your subscribers and manage your subscriber list conveniently in one location. You may also use it to import emails, clean email lists, track emails, and capture leads four times faster.

d) **Kenscio** - By enabling personalization and one-to-one connections, Kenscio's cutting-edge email marketing and Technology Solutions may help you manage email marketing campaigns. It offers real-time email personalisation, multichannel marketing, and social media monitoring.

e) **Juvlon** - Juvlon assists in creating professional-looking emails quickly. You may choose from its simple editors, template gallery, and customisable campaign features to make your emails more conversion-focused. Juvlon offers services encompassing email design, campaign reporting, contact list administration, email distribution, marketing automation, and SMS marketing.

f) **Vibe Mail** - Its sophisticated capabilities enable you to build, deliver, and track bulk email campaigns. Its cloud-based mass emailing solution provides the highest level of service reliability.

g) **Crux Mailer** is a cost-effective marketing solution for bulk email marketing requirements. Using its sophisticated HTML editor, you may quickly generate HTML (Hyper Text Markup Language) and text-based emails. It helps you find real-time open-and-click tracking information and lets you know who opens and reads your emails.

h) **Hems Mail** - With Hems Mail's SMTP server, you may send emails to your customers and stakeholders that can link back to your website and outbound bulk emails. You may receive assistance from Hems Mail with complete email marketing solutions for email design, sending, tracking, and audience targeting.

i) **CYBRIDGE** - It can assist you in turning contacts into customers with 100% managed email marketing by following up on your leads at the appropriate moment and ensuring conversions. CYBRIDGE enables you to track your visitors' emails, opens, clicks, and other types of activity. Personalised communications, mobile adaptability, and administration of the entire activity for you so that you may concentrate on your business are notable offerings. Additionally, CYBRIDGE supports you with tracking and analysis, bulk sending, and emailing that is spam-free and bounce-free.

j) **Brainpulse** - The business provides managed email marketing, which elevates your email campaigns and makes your messages more pertinent. Depending on your company's requirements, you may quickly select from the tailored email marketing plans. You may begin with planning and scheduling before moving on to email creation, sending, and measuring. It also offers email validation, data mining, and email marketing automation.

You may use any of the above ten email marketing tools in India. Some tools also have free versions for those on a tight budget.

Reference: [1] https://www.inventiva.co.in/trends/10-email-marketing-companies-india-2023/

Examples of Email Marketing

- **Zomato** - Its email marketing strategy has been a critical driver of its growth. They send highly personalised emails with pictures of delicious food and target specific user segments with relevant offers. This has helped them acquire new users and grow their business in new markets.

- **Netflix** - They send emails highlighting the latest featured movies and TV shows, encouraging new users to explore their platform regularly. They develop creative email campaigns to keep their recipients engaged. Based on their watch history, subscribers get a curated list of new shows they may be interested in through emails with the CTA (Call to Action), prompting you to watch that trailer and increasing engagement with their app.

- **Starbucks -** It has two email lists:

  a) The "My Starbucks Rewards" list is for program members.
  b) All contacts receive Starbucks news, announcements, and promotions. It dives into how users can gain 'rewards' to fuel that caffeine addiction.

  Each list sends an automated welcome email that nurtures the customer's relationship.

- **BookMyShow** - Sends weekly emails of events in the city, encouraging the users to open the app and explore, which is very handy, especially for selling movie tickets online. One example is when it sold over 15 million tickets for "Bahubali 2" [a Hindi movie] and contributed heavily to its overall business of over Rs 100 crore.

- **Indigo** - It has a regularly updated customer database and sends messages about offers, promotion schemes, and discount coupons directly to its email inboxes. They also email information on new route introductions, inflight magazines, and festival offers.

- **Myntra** - This is an online shopping platform that offers a seamless and convenient shopping experience. The company uses email marketing to engage customers by announcing new sales and discounts. They use a variety of email templates including abandoned cart emails, to encourage customers to complete their purchases with messages such as "You've left some great items in your cart, and we'd love for you to have them" or sending the items in the cart with prices and including a Call-to-Action 'Purchase' button. Additionally, it regularly dispatches newsletters containing details about new product launches, upcoming sales, and exclusive discounts.

Email marketing is beneficial as almost everyone with a digital presence monitors their emails daily. It is inexpensive, provides many advantages, such as brand awareness and visibility, and encourages users to visit the website through CTA prompts. It is very scalable. It is one of those marketing efforts with a more individual touch, creating a loyal and devoted customer base.

Chapter 7

PAID ADVERTISING - MAXIMISING ROI WITH EFFECTIVE ADVERTISING CAMPAIGNS

"Stopping advertising to save money is like stopping your watch to save time." **- Henry Ford**

Paid advertising is any form of advertising for which a marketer or company pays. Through paid ads, advertisers secure space on platforms catering to their target audience to promote their offerings. We will primarily look at digital paid ads as it has become crucial to have a digital presence in today's world.

In the digital realm, paid ads are often referred to as **PPC ("Pay Per Click")** advertising, but not all paid ads follow this model. These ads are usually showcased across platforms like Google search results, social media, and other websites, offering extensive reach and generating substantial ROI (Return on Investment).

Factors to consider before using Paid Ads

a) You should always budget your expenses, as paid ads can be expensive.

b) Check your ROI (Return on Investment) from your paid ads. ROI is the amount you earn from every dollar you spend on your ad campaign.

$$\textbf{Social media ROI \%} = \frac{\textbf{Earning - Costs}}{\textbf{Costs}} \times 100$$

Earnings include the revenue you have earned from your campaign.

Costs are your hours spent in strategising and making the ad content.

Basic steps, applicable to most digital paid ad platforms

1. Select an ad platform based on your audience's predominant presence and paid advertising objectives, and create your account there.

2. Craft your ad. Specify the target audience, determine the ad copy (content that prompts action), and upload accompanying visuals.

3. Establish your ad budget. Decide on your expenditure—whether daily, overall, or per ad.

4. Schedule the ad's display duration. Choose between specific periods or durations, such as two weeks or selected time slots.

5. Launch your ad. Platforms typically review ad content to ensure compliance with their guidelines.

6. When viewers meet your ad's criteria, an automated bidding process determines the ad display.

7. Payment occurs based on the agreed-upon terms, which may or may not be pay-per-click for all ads.

Different forms of Paid Advertising

Paid ads can take any of the following forms:

1) **Display Ads** - Display advertising aims to draw a specific audience to a website, social media platform, or other digital medium. These ads come in various formats, like text, videos, or images. Typically, they direct users to a landing page, encouraging specific actions like purchasing. Many display ads operate on a Pay-Per-Click (PPC) model, where marketers only incur charges when a user clicks on the ad.

2) **Social Media Ads**- Social media ads encompass promotional campaigns across diverse platforms like LinkedIn, Twitter, Facebook, and Instagram. Tailoring ads on LinkedIn assists in targeting B2B audiences, while Facebook and YouTube ads cater to both B2B and B2C audiences. These cost-effective ads enable access to a broad audience,

ensuring a favourable return on investment (ROI). They serve as an excellent choice for entering new markets.

3) **Video Ad** - The primary approach for businesses to engage potential customers involves video ads executed across diverse social media platforms such as Vimeo, YouTube, or Facebook. These ads serve to enhance customers' comprehension of products or services.

4) **Influencer marketing** - Advertisers often use popular personalities, known as "influencers," who have large following on social media platforms, to promote their products or services. These influencers can significantly impact sales through product placements, where they feature the product in their content, and endorsements. Make sure the influencer has content relevant to your product to establish credibility.

5) **Native advertising** - Native advertising involves promoting products in a manner that doesn't come across as a direct commercial to consumers. Native ads are usually sponsored content on a user's social media feed and do not disrupt the reader's browsing. Video native ads entertain the viewer while subtly dropping hints of a brand. They appear below or beside the article you have just read. They also appear as "in-feed" ads as a part of your news feeds on Facebook or Twitter.

6) **Retargeting/ Remarketing Ads** - Remarketing ads aim to re-engage with customers by targeting ads specifically at them. Retargeting ads, on the

other hand, are directed at individuals who have previously visited your website and potentially already exist as contacts in your database.

Such ads can generate higher conversions while lowering ad spending. Every successful business embraces this marketing strategy.

7) **Pay-Per-Click** - PPC (Pay-Per-Click) is an online advertising approach where advertisers exclusively pay for clicks generated by their ads. The ad may or may not be targeted at the keywords that a user searches for.

8) **Search Engine Marketing (SEM) -** Search engine marketing (SEM) is basically the practice of promoting websites by ensuring that the business's products are visible in search engine results pages (SERPs). In short, this means that when a customer searches for certain keywords on search engines, by using SEM, advertisers can ensure that customers will see your website among the first few search results.

This can include paid advertising or Search Engine Optimization (SEO). Paid advertising involves paying the search engine to feature your website as one of the top search results. It will have the 'Ad' or 'Sponsored' tag under the result. SEO refers to organic results, that is, "free" traffic, which is the result of providing relevant, useful content that ranks well on Google. In the SERP, these would show up after the paid results.

Advertisers select relevant keywords for their product, create ads, and determine their maximum cost per click and target locations. Google (or any other search engine) then uses an ad auction system where the advertisers bid on keywords that customers might enter when looking for certain products or services. Winning ads are then displayed on the SERP.

Some important points to note are:

- It is not only about who makes the highest bid but also about the relevance and quality of the ad content.

- Keywords selection - Choosing the right keywords is very important for SEM; hence, the business must identify exactly what words prospective customers might use to look for their product. Several online tools are available to help you generate keywords related to your business.

- Negative keywords - If a user has included a term that is not relevant to your product, they are likely not part of your target audience. E.g., if you sell baking goods and the entered search term is "cake recipe," they are probably not interested in buying your product.

- Some keywords are considered to have a high commercial intent, like 'buy', 'discount', and 'coupons'. It is more likely that such users will complete the purchase or desired action.

- Show ads only for inventory that is available.

- You can choose to link the ad to the page of your website that is most relevant instead of your homepage.

- When you are able to deliver what was advertised on your ad, like discounts or promotional sales, it is likely to increase your conversion rates.

- Fine-tune your ad copy until it achieves the expected results.

- Instead of marketing your product to everyone who may be interested in it, try to use market segmentation and reach customers who are sure of using your product.

Paid Advertising Pros and Cons

Pros:

1) **Instant results** - Allows advertisers to put their products in front of customers who are already motivated to make the purchase. Paid ads are the fastest way to reach your target audience. The intended audience can promptly view the ad and engage in actions like visiting your site or checking out your products.

2) **Audience-specific keywords** - If the right keywords are chosen based on your ad's theme and product line, the right audience can be targeted effectively. Opting for more specific keywords ensures your ad appears only for terms relevant to your business. Remember that if the keywords are too exact, you might not reach as many people as you'd like.

3) **Faster business growth** - Online shopping is very popular these days, so digital ads are a good way to reach your target audience. If you can advertise on

the right platforms, your reach will increase, resulting in more rapid business growth.

4) **Easily measurable** - Since you can measure each click on your ad, it is easy to calculate the revenue earned through the ad, and one can change the ad to get a better outcome depending on the revenue targeted. Tools like Google Analytics provide good insights into how your ad is doing and what improvements could be made.

5) **Market Segmentation** – This helps you understand what kind of people are looking for your products.

Cons:

1) **Cost** - Depending on the budget, paid ads could get expensive over time. Frequently monitoring the ad statistics and updating them accordingly may help in obtaining a good ROI.

2) **Competition** - Ensuring your product shows up at the top in auction-based ads could be expensive, given there is a lot of competition over popular keywords.

Most Popular Paid Ad Platforms

1) **Google Ads** - Google's paid advertising platform reaches a vast population and specific target audiences. You can create search ads, display ads, shopping ads, or YouTube ads. It provides diverse targeting options based on location, interests, purchasing intent, income, etc.

2) **YouTube Ads** - It allows you to pay to display your ad on viewers' YouTube pages. You can create a business account and post ads on the platform in different formats, like bumper ads (short-video format) or discover ads (shows up as YouTube suggestions on user pages).

3) **Facebook Ads** - Your ads can reach Facebook's millions of users through its Ads feature. You can target them based on likes, demographics, and whether they follow your competitors. Ad options include boosted posts, video ads, image ads, stories ads, slideshow ads (group images to create a short video), messenger ads, poll ads (add a poll to engage with users), and instant experience ads (use multimedia to allow users to browse product lists).

4) **LinkedIn Ads** - You can effectively target business users on mobile or desktop apps based on job titles or industries by creating various ad types like text ads, lead ads (allowing users to fill in their details), sponsored messaging (in users' app inboxes), and dynamic ads tailored to individual users.

5) **Instagram Ads** - It has one of the most diverse ad offerings. You can promote your products on Instagram stories or post video ads to attract more followers. You can create image ads, video ads, carousel ads (multiple images/videos in a single ad), stories ads, collection ads (e-commerce businesses can add product lists for users to browse), explore ads (appear in the Explore section), reel ads (videos up to 60 seconds long). It is an ideal platform for any business.

6) **Twitter Ads** - It offers several ad types, like promoted ads, follower ads, ads in video content on Twitter, Twitter takeovers or live ads. Make Twitter ads interactive by adding polls, conversation buttons, website links, and branded notifications for more engagement.

7) **Pinterest Ads** - If you're in the creative industry, Pinterest is the perfect platform. Its visual ads seamlessly integrate with its posts and come in various formats—standard pins, carousel pins, video pins, and shopping pins. The platform provides adaptable tools and personalised targeting options that enable businesses to create ads prompting specific actions, such as app installations or enhancing brand recognition.

8) **Amazon Ads** - Amazon ads allow you to reach high-intent purchasers. Because Amazon targets users who are already ready to buy, ads can have a higher ROI. Ad types on Amazon include product ads, store ads, audio ads, video ads, and programmatic advertising. Since Amazon has hosting services, streaming services, music platforms, and Alexa, it can reach a wider audience.

9) **Microsoft Ads** - Microsoft Ads, also known as Bing Ads, offers a service enabling users to explore Yahoo and Bing search engines. These ads operate on the PPC advertising model.

Examples of Best Ad Campaigns in India

Ad campaigns attract billions of viewers. Companies spend 7- 8% of their revenue on advertisements, sometimes even more. Some popular ads of companies include Parle's 'Why is Melody so Chocolaty', Amul's 'Doodh Doodh' jingle, Maggi's 'Maggi Maggi' jingle, and the most loved Nirma's 'Sabki Pasand' jingle, which have made a great impact on their audience across all age groups.

1. Meesho's Sahi Sahi Lagaya Hain Campaign

Before the festive season, Meesho, an e-commerce platform, launched its 'Sahi Sahi Lagaya Hain' campaign to attract customers with a wide range of products at affordable prices. The recurring line **"Sahi Sahi Lagaya Hain"** captured the attention of many people in India, as people use this phrase while negotiating with vendors. Meesho gave assurance of a "one-stop solution" at the right price. Its social media campaign went so viral that it became a prime source of memes.

2. Tata Tea Premium's 'Kadak Mumbai Ke Liye Kadak Chai' Campaign

2021 was the best year for Tata Tea Premium's social media marketing. Tata Tea Premium launched a marketing campaign that broke all stereotypes of the professional people of Mumbai. This one-minute video ad tries to show the 'Kadak' (vital) spirit of Mumbai, whose residents are perceived to be detached or indifferent towards others. The ad shows how Mumbai is different from other cities with its fast-paced, no-nonsense, busy lives led by its citizens. It also has a passionate spirit of humanity and empathy during times of need. In the ad, a restaurant manager rejects the employment of her employee's brother because he does not have the required skills but invites a group of underprivileged people who are taking shelter outside her restaurant for food, showing her large-heartedness. With the catchphrase **'Kadak Mumbai Ke Liye Kadak Chai'**, this social media campaign tries to link this 'Kadak' spirit of Mumbai to its 'Kadak chai'.

3. Tanishq's 'When It Rings True' Campaign

Tanishq Jewellery launched an ad campaign, **"When It Rings True,"** with the unique concept of cherishing a bond between a couple. The social media campaign features a couple discussing their wedding engagement. The female lead is sceptical about her decision, and later, she confirms the engagement after realising how correct they are for each other when the male lead addresses what she was concerned about and eases her mind. With this ad, Tanishq tried to show that when it 'rings true' for the couple, they can strengthen the bond with a beautiful Tanishq diamond ring. This marketing campaign shows romantic and candid emotions in the video ad, hence connecting effortlessly with its target audience.

4. Mohey Manyavar's 'Kanyadaan' Campaign

Mohey Manyavar rolled out an ad campaign for its social media marketing that shined a new light on old Indian Hindu wedding rituals and customs. Weddings are unions of two families, and traditions are integral, especially 'Kanyadaan' (the father giving away the daughter), which has an emotional touch. This social media campaign promotes a progressive mindset by showing how daughters are not something that can be given away ('Daan') and instead should be respected ('Maan'), hence suggesting that this ritual be changed from 'KanyaDaan' to 'KanyaMaan'. Though media trolls requested to boycott the ad due to what they felt was an outdated practice, this ad changed their perspective on the rituals and customs.

5. Cadbury's Good Luck Girls Campaign

Cadbury rolled out an ad campaign for its social media marketing with a particular thought. This marketing campaign recreates their own famous and iconic *'Asli Swad Zindagi Ka'* ad with a different perspective. The ***"Good Luck Girls"*** campaign admires girls and honours their success as powerful role models. In 1990, their iconic ad featured a girl cheering and running on the pitch to celebrate a male cricketer striking a shot. Cadbury recreated this ad with the roles interchanged, wherein now a man runs onto the field to celebrate a great shot by a female cricketer. This is an excellent ad campaign by Cadbury and was received very well by the audience. Cadbury's social media campaign proved its tagline, **Kuch Accha Ho Jaye, Kuch Meetha Ho Jaye.**

6. Amazon Pay's Ab Har Din Hua Aasan Campaign

Amazon Pay has focused on the journey of payments from cash to digital platforms. This social media campaign tries to show that payments with Amazon Pay are convenient and easy for both the customer and the business owner. The company has launched the **Ab Har Din Hua Aasan** campaign, which shows how the digital age has become a significant part of day-to-day life, money, and business deals. After the demonetization process, the importance of cash payments decreased, and digital payments have become an integral part of the Indian people's lives. It further promotes the digital services of Amazon Pay and showcases that transactions through Amazon Pay are instant and easy.

These advertisements have managed to change the perspectives of many people worldwide.

In conclusion, paid advertising refers to a marketing effort where you spend money on an ad campaign to reach a target audience more effectively. You can gain customers instantly and improve your profits. Depending on your budget, you can use this strategy to get potential customers quickly and build brand awareness.

Chapter 8

CRAFTING YOUR UNIQUE SELLING PROPOSITION - STANDING OUT FROM THE CROWD

"If you don't distinguish yourself from the crowd, you'll just be the crowd."
- Rebecca Mark

A Unique Selling Proposition (USP) is a marketing statement that differentiates your products or services from those of your competitors. It should offer something competitors cannot offer and always attract new customers. Crafting a good USP and delivering on it will make your existing customers repeatedly return to you for your products and services. In short, the USP is what you believe your business is good at. For example, most owners of Maruti Suzuki cars will tell you that one of the main factors that influenced their purchase decision was good mileage and availability of service centres, which is the USP of this manufacturer.

Four USP Categories for Differentiating Your Product

Your brand's USP can be along the following lines:

1) **Price** - Are we selling our product or services at a lower, more competitive cost, or are they linked to an activity-based cost (like machine setup costs or consumed power)?

2) **Quality** - Are we providing higher-quality products or services than our competitors?

3) **Convenience** - Can we deliver to customers faster by keeping supply points at key locations or by providing a product value proposition summarising why customers would choose your product over competitors?

4) **Differentiation** - Can we define why our product differs from others or how our product's features have something unique to offer compared to others?

Steps to Create a Unique Selling Proposition

A strong USP is essential to make your product irresistible to your customers. It should address a specific need experienced by your ideal customer. Let us look into the steps for creating a strong USP:

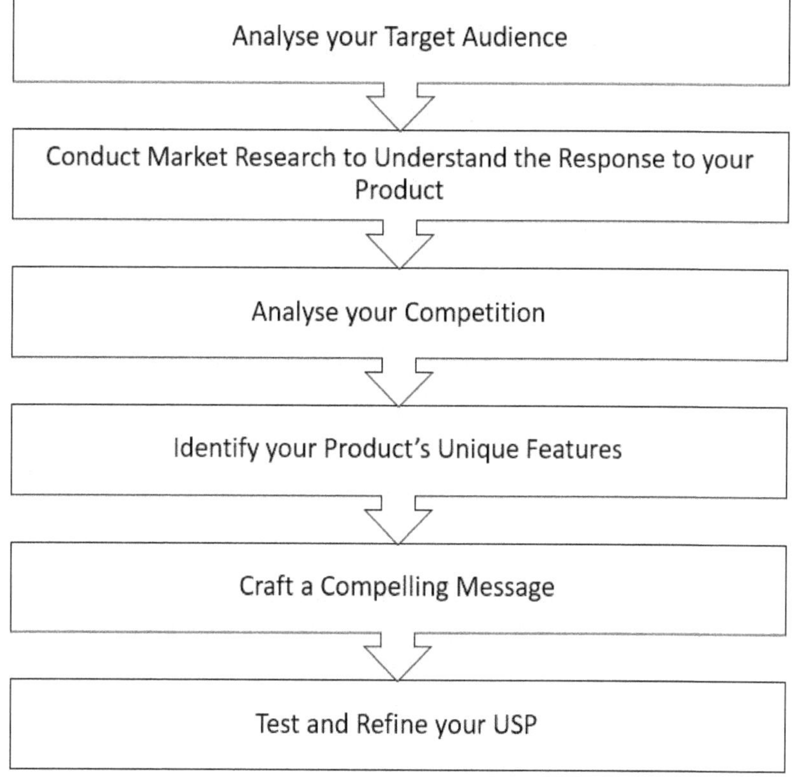

1) Target Audience

While creating the product, you must have had a particular group of people in mind. Understanding them would be the starting point for USP creation. Analyse what you know about this audience and why they buy your offerings; for example, is your service time-saving for them, or maybe they trust your expertise?

2) Conduct Market Research

Research your potential consumers and understand their needs and preferences. Consider conducting interviews with a group of customers to gather valuable feed back. Use this information to create a campaign sheet that aligns with the product details and addresses the requirements of your target audience. This sheet aims to address questions such as:

- What problem does your product solve for your customer?
- How are they using your product?
- How does it affect their experience?
- What motivated their decision to buy your product?
- What differentiates you from the competition?

It would help if you carried out a similar exercise for your competitors to understand why some customers prefer them. Once you have identified the strengths and weaknesses of your competitors, you are better placed to position yourself in your market.

3) Analyse the Competition

You should look closely at the customers buying from competitors and find out why they prefer their products. Also, if you can identify the competitors' USP and value proposition, you can work out ways to prove your products differ.

4) Identify your Unique Selling Points

Listing down the unique selling points of your product will assist you in delivering an efficient campaign. Now that you know the market size and competition, listing down the niche offerings of your product can be a significant differentiator. Assessing your strengths and weaknesses also aids in monitoring potential opportunities and threats to your growth. Keeping tabs on your strengths and weaknesses can also help you monitor potential opportunities and threats to your development.

5) Craft a Compelling Message

To keep your competitors engaged, your USP should be crisp, straightforward, and written in simple language to make your offering innovative, beneficial, and worthwhile. Try to limit it to one sentence, and that should be appealing to your customers so they buy your product. You can use real-life examples to highlight the merits of your product. Using videos, graphics, or testimonials from customers who have had a positive experience using your products can add immense value to your USP messages.

6) Test and refine your USP

After unveiling your USP to customers, seek their feedback on their experience with your products or services post-launch. Avoid complex language that may hinder customers from connecting with your brand. Keep your USP concise and impactful. Conduct an A/B test by presenting two different USPs on your company's landing page to two different groups of people ('A' and 'B') and selecting the one that resonates most with your audience.

Examples of Successful USP's

1) **Canva:** <u>"Empowering the world to design"</u>

   Its service primarily focuses on streamlining graphic design processes to empower anyone to design beautifully at lower prices. Its USP conveys what makes the service unique and better with fewer words. Some of its unique offerings captured by the USP are:

   a) Drag and drop features for elements in ready-made templates make it easy for people with no design knowledge to use

   b) With low prices, more people can afford it.

   c) Has a competitive advantage in the market with pre-made templates for different social media platforms and various types of content (like invites, posters, and videos). Users can simply modify existing templates to create their own content.

2) **Nike:** <u>"Bring inspiration and innovation to every athlete in the world."</u>

   Nike hires top professional athletes to promote their products. Their campaign, "If you have a body, you're an athlete," reinforces the following ideas:

   a) It widens the buyer persona to non-athletes by saying that anyone with the right footwear can potentially be an athlete.

b) It gives the idea that the buyer is getting shoes endorsed by athletes at affordable prices.

c) It shows that the company always supports sportspeople.

3) **Coca-Cola:** <u>"Refresh the world; Make a difference."</u>

Coca-Cola highlights its vision of refreshing people with its product while maintaining a sustainable business and making a difference in the community. Their ad campaigns revolve around celebration and emotions, positioning them as a brand that is a source of happiness and enjoyment.

4) **Starbucks:** <u>"Expect more than a coffee."</u>

The success of Starbucks goes beyond coffee; it is also about getting people to connect with positive things in their daily lives, for some people, it could be a good chat with friends over tasty coffee. Starbucks's USP is a great coffee along with cafes with a good ambience where people can hang out with friends or bring their laptops and work peacefully.

5) **Domino's Pizza:** <u>"You get fresh, hot pizza delivered to your door in 30 minutes or less, or it's free."</u>

In a crowded pizza market, Domino's came up with the famous USP of delivering food within 30 minutes, which made it a preferred pizza outlet amongst buyers.

6) **IKEA:** <u>"To create a better everyday life for the many people"</u>

IKEA's USP is to provide home furnishing products at low prices so more people can afford to buy them.

Their furniture has an element of DIY (Do It Yourself), making it convenient for customers to assemble or transport their products, as well as a sustainable angle as the furniture is made from engineered wood. Even as a late entrant, IKEA's USP has helped it reach a wide audience.

Chapter 9

NURTURING RELATIONSHIPS - BUILDING CUSTOMER LOYALTY AND RETENTION

The more you engage with customers, the clearer things become and the easier it is to determine what you should be doing." **- John Russell**

In a growing business, there can be times when the company suffers a downslide due to various reasons, like heavy competition or geopolitical situations. Businesses that have strong customer relations tend to grow. They will always have a solid, loyal customer base that stands with them in adversaries.

What is a Customer Relationship?

Customer relationship refers to the company's strategies to build and improve the customer experience. When you develop a strong relationship with your customer, you end up with a loyal and permanent customer. In the age of increasing competition, every customer interaction should leave a positive impression on them.

Adidas is an excellent example of solid customer relationship management. It gives outstanding services, communicates well, offers personalised services, always works on customer feedback, and consistently offers reward programs to its users. Adidas has committed to ending plastic waste through Prime Green fabrics made of 100% recycled polyester, helping Adidas retain its target audience and loyal customers.

Why is Building Customer Relationships Important?

Building a good rapport with your prospects and customers is one of the vital things every business needs, and helps in -

- Gaining Customer Loyalty

  When you respond quickly to customer needs, you have a loyal customer base that will always choose you over your competitors and can become your brand ambassador. Remembering seemingly small details like their birthdays can go a long way in maintaining good relations with customers.

- Maximising ROI of marketing campaigns

Retaining your existing customers is always more important than converting new ones, as existing customers purchased your products for a reason and are likely to buy them again. Listening to your customers' needs and accommodating them whenever possible is essential. When choosing between two similar products, customers will choose the one where they had a better experience over the other.

- Increasing Customer Lifetime Value (CLV)

When you have developed a loyal customer base, you have more extensive sales, as customers are ready to pay more for your goods or services and will always trust your brand performance.

Eleven Factors to Build Long-standing Customer Relationships

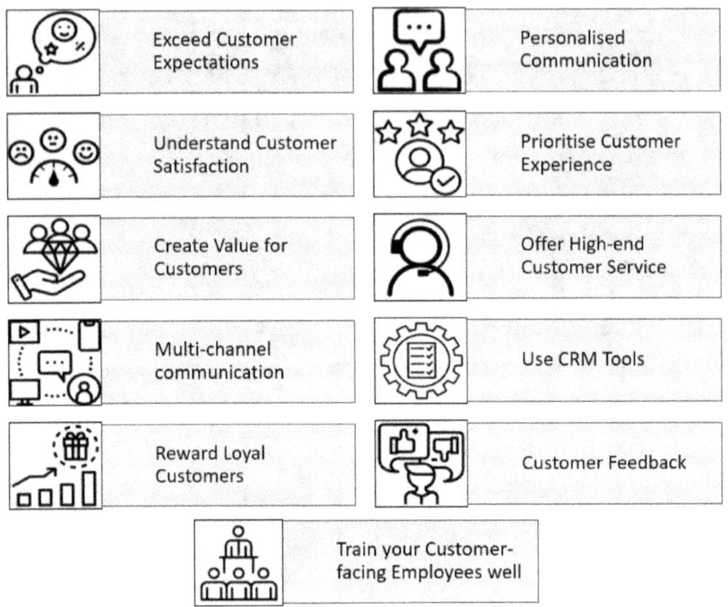

1) Exceed customer service expectations

a) **Deliver real-time support:** Your support teams should have a "live chat" with your customers to understand and deliver proactive support to them.

b) **Connect with your customers:** Empower your support team to meet your customers directly to understand their needs and feedback.

c) **Get customer feedback regularly:** Make your customers feel special by taking their feedback on the services provided. Send them "Thank You" notes and connect with them regularly by sending newsletters and updates on new happenings in your company.

Holiday Inn Mumbai sets a great example of creating memorable customer service. One of my friends had left his favourite Parker pen in the hotel room during his stay there. Before he could call the hotel, he received a call from them confirming his pen was in safe custody. Your loyalty to such companies always increases with such acts.

2) Personalise your communication

Connecting with your customers personally is the key to establishing a long and trustworthy relationship with your business. It increases loyalty, drives in more customers, and increases revenue. Some ways to do this are:

- Match your tone with the customers' personality. Understand whether your customers prefer a short or a long conversation and accordingly adjust your interaction.
- Use live assistant tools like co-browsing and video chat to connect in real-time. Sharing the screen is an even better option. With screen sharing during video calls, you can engage with your customers more personally and provide an in-person experience virtually.
- Listen to the customers' preferences, request them to share their preferred contact channels, and understand how to address them, which will aid in building a more robust bond with your customers.
- Send anniversary wishes over email and personalised incentives on birthdays and other

significant dates with discount coupons or gifts to create a loyal customer for you.

3) Understand Customer Satisfaction

When you understand a customer's needs, you boost customer satisfaction rates. Customers look forward to being valued, need immediate resolution of their problems, and want assurance that the problem will not repeat. It would help if you always kept your eyes and ears open for customer issues and instantly delivered the right solution.

The main benefits of understanding customer satisfaction are:

a) Loyal customers: A satisfied customer becomes your brand ambassador and helps grow revenue.
b) Brand Advocacy: Your customers' success stories can be captured and advocated for in your brand statements.

Tupperware, a company that manufactures storage containers for the kitchen and home, is known for its high quality and longevity. They offer a lifetime warranty for their container lids, making them a preferred storage container for the kitchen and home, and they have developed a loyal customer base.

4) Prioritise Customer Experience

You should always aim to build a long-term relationship in which you will have loyal and permanent customer who will also become your brand ambassador. Build a consistent customer experience by rewarding loyal customers with awards, gifts and concessions.

Vistara Airlines rewards their Gold and Platinum customers with various incentives, like a separate check-in counter, lounge entry (with an assistant in the Platinum category), flexibility in changing flights on the day of travel, and special flight seats, which results in the customer feeling essential and ensures their loyalty.

5) Create Value for Customers

a) **Look into your customers' needs:** Meet your major customers personally, understand their needs, and assist them in that direction.

b) **Build customer groups:** Form groups of your customers to discuss with them over a video call or an offline seminar and showcase your products and services to get their feedback. You can also create education groups to help your customers use your products best.

c) **Highlight your cost:** When explaining the pricing of your product to your customer, it is essential to be transparent and clear about what they're paying for and what the costs entail. Holding open discussions with them may ensure they are ready to pay a higher cost to avail of your better service. For example, many mutual fund managers clearly state where they will invest customer funds, whether in large-cap, mid-cap, or small-cap. They may also mention the companies they will be investing in, thereby creating more value for customers to encourage them to invest in your funds.

d) **Enhance knowledge of your customer:** Use various marketing ploys to line up your prospects. In the refrigeration segment (crowded market), **Voltas**, a known brand of the Tata group, educated customers about their refrigerators using "PUF" (Polyurethane Foam) insulations that had high thermal properties but allowed for very minimal air infiltration, which, in turn, resulted in increased revenue earnings, eventually leading to other competitors also highlighting the same.

6) Offer High-end Customer Service and Position a service franchisee.

Having dealers in areas where users are primarily present always increases your brand value. You should patiently hear your customers' problems and offer solutions immediately. In case of delays, you should offer apologies to customers with sincerity. Remember the **Maruti** Car advertisement for their service station located in remote and mountainous terrain? Customers prefer Maruti cars for the location of service stations in all key areas.

7) Communicate with your customers using various channels

It is important to remain accessible to your customers so they can easily reach you with questions and issues. Always check with your customers to see whether email, live chat, social channels, text messages, or any other form of communication can best reach them. You should:

- Understand the needs of the target audience.

- Use the proper communication channels to provide the best experience for your customers.
- Use conversational engagement across channels through which customers reach out to you.
- Use of multi-channel strategy: Create content specifically tailored to suit each channel. Ensure that the content is different but the message is consistent.

Examples of Multichannel Marketing

- **Amazon** sells its products through its website, mobile application, brick-and-mortar stores, websites, social media advertisements, and television commercials. It creates a seamless customer experience.

- **Nike** uses brick-and-mortar stores worldwide, an e-commerce website, direct mail catalogues, and social media accounts.

- **Pepperfry** is an online furniture store with brick-and-mortar stores that reaches customers via online channels and concept-based retail studio outlets. They also offer live video calls, customer support, and consultation to enable direct and personalised customer interactions. They provide features such as 3D visualisations, virtual try-ons (allowing you to place the product in your home using augmented reality), and product demos, which help their customers visualise how the products will look in their homes.

- **Lenskart** recently added a massive chain of stores for its offline presence and has also created a 3D virtual trial room on its mobile app that allows customers to try out different spectacle frames virtually.

In addition to marketing, having a multi-channel presence can help offer customers different ways of reaching you. Customers often have long waiting times just getting a customer representative on the phone, which can get frustrating; hence, having multiple options can help you show that you respect their time.

8) Use of Customer Relationship Management Tools

CRMs are powerful tools that help record factors such as customer activity on your app, product choices, spending patterns, location, age, and gender, which assist in profiling your customers' buying habits.

It helps in:

- Knowing your customers
- Segmenting the customer base
- Being clear about customer needs and interests
- Retaining the customer base
- Ensuring quick customer communication

Some examples of CRM tools are Salesforce, HubSpot, Pipedrive, and Insightly.

9) Reward Loyal Customers

Loyal customers are your Brand Ambassadors.

Reward them by:

- Offering incentives: Discounts, free products, festival discounts
- Multichannel service: Offer premium services like co-browsing, video chat and chatbot support and telephone support
- Early access to reward programs, thereby giving them something exclusive

For example, many airlines offer their loyal customers:

- Early boarding on preferred seats
- Lounge Facility
- Option of changing their schedules
- Particular preferences while refunding or reorganising their tours

10) Customer Feedback

Obtain genuine feedback on your product's performance by collecting feedback and acting on it.

a) Establish a regular feedback mechanism with your target audience.
b) Post-service calls, ask for feedback, and also discuss the service report.
c) Obtain customer feedback reports, internally discuss them in your company with the respective departments, and take preventive or suggestive actions.

11) Train your customer-facing employees well

Your customer relationship managers and teams should be well-versed with the product, and have excellent communication skills and patience while dealing with customers. Soft skills like 'active listening' (showing an active interest in what your customer is saying), professional behaviour, and a problem-solving attitude should be developed in employees working on customer relationships. They should have enough knowledge about the product to resolve problems, preferably within the first call from a customer. Build customer trust by being transparent with them, for example, by informing them of potential delays in their orders, which helps them plan their activities accordingly. Provided it doesn't happen often, they will appreciate your honesty. Invest in regular employee training and show your appreciation to bring out the best in your employees.

Maintaining a great customer experience and ensuring customer satisfaction are necessary for good customer relationships. Your business should deliver a stellar customer experience, influencing the customers' buying decisions in your favour.

Chapter 10

SCALING UP - STRATEGIES FOR SUSTAINED GROWTH AND LONG-TERM SUCCESS

"It's not the strongest of the species that survive, nor the most intelligent, but the one most responsive to change." - **Charles Darwin**

Scaling up a business and continuously sustaining growth efforts and results is a big challenge for any company and its owners. The leadership team must ensure business growth occurs without compromising on quality or increasing costs. The business should gradually increase its infrastructure and skilled workforce to cater to the increased sales volumes while steadily aiming to reduce costs.

Steps to Scale up the Businesses

1) **Define your growth goals and vision roadmap**
   a) Set up "SMART" (Specific, Measurable, Achievable, Relevant, and Time-bound) goals that align with your objectives for the next five years.
   b) Break up each year's plans into:
      i) Business as usual (BAU)
      ii) Business from new products
   c) Draw your Key Performance Indicators (KPIs) that reflect growth drivers in each business.
   d) Figure out the actions needed to achieve your growth parameters.
   e) Break down your goals into smaller milestones, thereby leading to big goals being planned.

2) **Establish a Growth team**
   a) Create a dedicated, cross-functional team that can execute your growth strategy.
   b) Pick up growth-minded people from each function to form a robust cross-functional team.
   c) Create a culture of growth that encourages collaboration, experimentation, learning, and adaptation to new ideas and challenges.
   d) Define a straightforward growth process for your cross-functional team, clearly defining their roles and expected outcomes.
   e) Provide the tools, resources, and incentives that enable your growth team to perform effectively and efficiently.

3) **Experiment with new ways to improve the growth rate**
   a) Test your assumptions, validate your ideas, and discover new opportunities.
   b) Follow a structured, data-driven approach to design, run, and analyse your experiments.
   c) Take feedback from stakeholders and refine your experiments to make them growth-oriented.
   d) The team should adopt a growth mindset that embraces failure, curiosity, and creativity.

4) **Align and integrate all teams and functions**
   a) Create harmony with your teams and functions.
   b) Align product development, marketing, sales, customer services, and operations in line with your growth plans.
   c) Ensure growth strategies align with your brand identity, value proposition, customer acceptance, and competitiveness.
   d) Upgrade your systems, platforms, and channels to align with your growth.

5) **Monitoring Growth results**
   a) Monitor and evaluate your growth results regularly and systematically.
   b) Run the above data along with your KPIs and identify the high and low spots. Work on the soft spots to bridge the gaps and achieve your benchmarks.
   c) Assess each individual's contribution to the team and align them with the devised growth strategy, train them accordingly, or look for new resources.

d) When two resources work for 8 hours each, the total time dedicated to the project is 16 hours. By monitoring outcomes based on this perspective, the growth percentage significantly surpasses a collaborative effort.

e) Be flexible, agile, and responsive to your growth challenges and opportunities.

6) Adapt to a changed environment and customer needs

a) Reviewing what works and does not work to adapt to changes is crucial for business survival.

b) Adapt and evolve your growth strategy based on your results and learnings.

c) Update, refine, and revise your goals and metrics based on your performance and impact.

Examples of Companies Successful in Scaling Up

1) **Zerodha:**

   An Indian financial services company (a member of NSE, BSE, and MCX) started in 2010 and offers brokerage for free equity investments, retail, institutional broking, currencies, and commodity trading. Their business model is "Low Margin and High-Volume Target." The model does not charge brokerage fees for equity investments and only charges a small fee for other services. As a result, the number of active clients increased significantly and helped create brand awareness, increasing profitability. Their app's user-friendly design gives users a great trading experience. As a part of scaling up, they also launched products like mutual fund investments, commodities trading, and currency trading, allowing customers to use a single platform for all their investment needs. It has grown its revenue from Rs 800 Cr in FY 2019 to Rs 5459 Cr in FY 2023, with a margin from Rs 400 Cr in FY 2019 to Rs 2354 Cr in FY 2023. *(Source: HDFC Securities).*

2) **Reliance Retail:**

It operates in consumer electronics, fashion, lifestyle, grocery, Pharma, and connectivity consumption baskets. As of 2023, it has over 245,000 employees at 18000 store locations in 7000 towns. Apart from physical stores, the company sells products through its e-commerce channels. It quickly established enduring connections with millions of customers by offering limitless choices, exceptional value propositions, top-notch quality, and unparalleled experiences across its retail outlets. For FY 23, its gross revenue stood at Rs 2.6 L Cr, and net profit surged 30% to Rs 9181 Cr *(Source: Financial Express, Business Today).*

3) **Chai Sutta Bar:**

It started as a popular Indian Chai franchise established in 2016 and has grown to a Rs. 100 crore turnover with zero market investment. The cafe has expanded to more than 195 cities in India and has also opened outlets in Nepal, the UAE, and Oman. Chai Sutta Bar made a strategic choice by adopting the franchise business model, characterised by lower capital expenditure and higher returns, thus making the Chai franchise a highly sought-after option for aspiring entrepreneurs seeking to partner with a reputable brand *(Source: Financial Express).*

4) **Flipkart:**

It operates as an online marketplace that connects buyers and sellers across India. The company generates revenue through commission-based fees, logistics and fulfilment services, advertising, subscription-based services, and financial services.

How Flipkart functions:

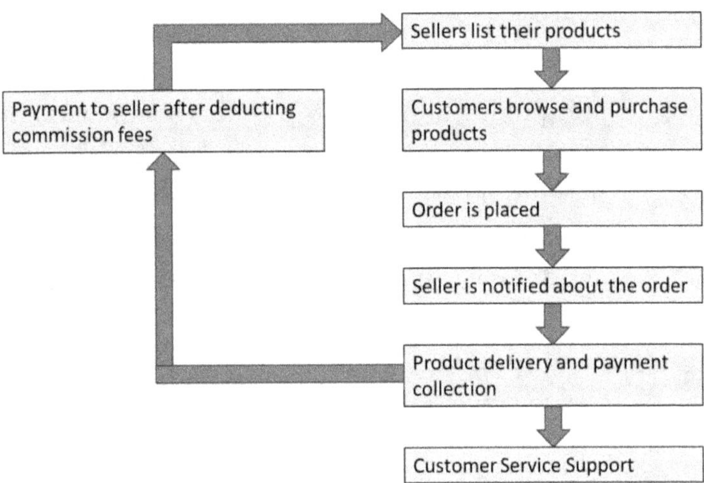

It offers customers a smooth shopping experience while generating revenue streams for its sellers and partners.

Flipkart's fiscal year 2022-2023 revenue is USD 15 billion, an increase from USD 10 billion in the 2021-2022 fiscal year. For scaling up, Flipkart enhances assisted e-commerce interventions like live commerce (hosting live streamed events where hosts or influencers showcase products in real-time) and video commerce (multimedia content seamlessly integrating product links). Expanding its audiobook library will be the focus area in 2023 *(Source: Business Line).*

In conclusion, while Scaling Up a business, consider the following tips:

1) **Rethink your brand:** Rapid growth demands attracting new customers and retaining the existing ones. Look for content-based marketing instead of direct marketing in a local area.

2) **Take Advice:** Before scaling up, seek advice from your professional network and friends. Look into similar companies that have grown fast and learn from them on what areas they have done well and their mistakes.

3) **Organisation restructuring:** Expand your organisation structure to scale up your business. You need to introduce new levels of management for **HR, IT** or other functions to ensure the company grows. Establishing a clear hierarchy and departmental responsibilities is essential before the business outgrows its current structure.

CONCLUSION: YOUR JOURNEY BEGINS

"Good marketing makes the company look smart. Great marketing makes the customer feel smart." - **Joe Chernov**

Congratulations on completing this comprehensive journey through the world of marketing! As you've discovered, marketing is a dynamic and ever-evolving field, filled with opportunities for growth, creativity, and impact.

Throughout this book, we've covered the essential principles, strategies, and tactics that will help you fast-track your marketing career. We began by looking at Marketing Mixes and how they serve as the starting point to understand customers' needs and position our offering accordingly. This will help build a strong brand identity and define how the market should perceive your brand. Next, we did a deep dive into how to find and connect with your target audience and how to pull them to your product by creating content strategies for different avenues like social media, email-based marketing, or paid advertising. Further, we discussed how to create a USP to make your product a unique offering in the market. We also hopefully gained some insight into maintaining a positive relationship with customers. Lastly, we looked at some strategies to scale up your business by 'zooming out' your focus and looking at the big picture to get ideas for sustained growth.

Whether you're a complete newbie or someone looking to refresh their knowledge, you now possess the tools to become a Marketing Ninja. But remember, this isn't the end; it's only the beginning of your marketing adventure. The marketing landscape constantly shifts, and staying up-to-date with the latest trends and technologies will be critical to your success. Marketing is a journey, not a destination. Keep learning, experimenting, and adapting to the ever-changing digital and consumer landscape.

Here are a few key takeaways to keep in mind as you embark on your marketing career:

1. **Be Inquisitive:** The marketing world is full of innovations and trends. Embrace your curiosity and never stop learning.

2. **Don't be afraid to say, 'I don't know':** Technology is constantly evolving, so don't feel bad

accepting when you are unaware of new concepts; instead, learn more about it. With your marketing experience, you will discover and explore new avenues.

3. **Make the most of your Data Ally:** Data-driven decisions are the foundation of successful marketing. Use analytics to refine your strategies.

4. **Creativity Matters:** While data is crucial, creativity sets you apart. Don't be afraid to think outside the box and experiment with new ideas.

5. **Test, Learn and Adapt:** The best marketers constantly test and refine their strategies. Be prepared to adapt to new ideas when necessary.

6. **Networking with Customers is Key:** Build a solid online and offline professional network. Connections can open doors and provide valuable insights.

7. **Be Patient:** Success in marketing takes time, and not everything you try will work instantly. Please don't get discouraged by setbacks; use them as opportunities to learn and grow.

As you venture into the marketing world armed with the knowledge from this book, remember that becoming a proper marketing Ninja is a journey of continuous improvement and adaptation. The skills and insights you've gained here will serve as a solid foundation, but the path you carve for yourself is entirely your own. So, go out there, embrace the challenges, and make your mark in the marketing world. Your journey is just beginning, and the possibilities are endless.

Thank you for joining me on this adventure, and I wish you all the best in your marketing career. May you become the Marketing Ninja you aspire to be!